21st Century Skills
Realising Our Potential

Individuals, Employers, Nation

department for
education and skills
creating opportunity, releasing potential, achieving excellence

HM TREASURY

DWP Department for
Work and Pensions

21st Century Skills
Realising Our Potential

Individuals, Employers,

Presented to Parliament by
the Secretary of State for Education and Skills
by Command of Her Majesty
July 2003

Cm 5810   £24.00

Contents

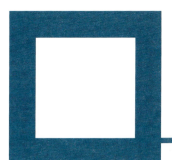

Foreword to the Skills Strategy

1. The skills of our people are a vital national asset. Skills help businesses achieve the productivity, innovation and profitability needed to compete. They help our public services provide the quality and choice that people want. They help individuals raise their employability, and achieve their ambitions for themselves, their families and their communities.

2. Sustaining a competitive, productive economy which delivers prosperity for all requires an ever growing proportion of skilled, qualified people. We will not achieve a fairer, more inclusive society if we fail to narrow the gap between the skills-rich and the skills-poor.

3. In addition, as the Prime Minister and the Chancellor said in setting out the Government's position on the single currency, skills underpin labour market flexibility, which is an important part of the assessment for deciding whether to join the Euro.

4. Increased flexibility is necessary to ensure that the economy could respond quickly and efficiently to changes in economic conditions inside the single currency area, should the Government conclude that the economic tests for entry have been met and recommend entry to the British people. An important dimension of that flexibility, identified in the EMU assessment, is the extent to which the supply of skills in the labour market matches the skills that are in demand from employers, and the efficiency with which mechanisms are in place to eliminate mismatches in the demand and supply of different skills when they emerge.

5. Across the European Union, the importance of skills has been recognised in the economic reform agenda agreed at Lisbon in 2000. The UK is a strong supporter of that agenda. Many of the topics addressed in this White Paper are issues of shared concern for all European countries. As well as setting out a national Skills Strategy, this document is a contribution to the work we are engaged in with our European partners

in tackling the challenges of skills and mobility across the Union, where it is vital that we identify best practice and share our experiences.

6.   We all know that skills matter. But we also know that as a nation we do not invest as much in skills as we should. Compared with other countries, we perform strongly in some areas, such as higher education. But we have major shortfalls in other areas such as the broad foundation skills needed for sustainable employment. The distribution of skills is uneven across the population. Far too many young people and adults are hampered by their lack of skills from getting secure, well paid jobs and all of the social and personal benefits that go with them.

7.   This is a national problem, but it also has to be addressed at both the regional and local level. Variations in the skills base of different regions are a major factor in explaining regional variations in productivity. The problems and priorities of one region are not the same as those encountered in another. Addressing these will require maximum flexibility and discretion at the regional and local level to innovate, respond to local conditions and meet differing consumer demands.

8.   We are under no illusion about the scale of the challenge. To raise our skill levels to compete with the best in the world requires millions of people, as employers, employees and individual learners, to see skills, training and qualifications as helping them to realise their goals in life and at work.

9.   This Skills Strategy aims to address that challenge. Our ambition is to ensure that employers have the right skills to support the success of their businesses and organisations, and individuals have the skills they need to be both employable and personally fulfilled.

10.   Success will not come quickly. This is an agenda for sustained effort over the long term, through to 2010 and beyond. It will not be gained through piecemeal initiatives. What is needed is a sustained and co-ordinated effort. By building upon what is already there and setting a framework within which the various players are clear about their contribution, we can make much faster progress towards the shared objective.

11.   To achieve that, we need to act in five key areas:

- We must put employers' needs for skills centre stage, managing the supply of training, skills and qualifications so that it responds directly to those needs.

- We must raise ambition in the demand for skills. We will only achieve increased productivity and competitiveness if more employers and more employees are encouraged and supported to make the necessary investment in skills. We need a new social partnership with employers and unions, and a much stronger focus on driving up skills and productivity in each sector of the economy and in each region.

- We must motivate and support many more learners to re-engage in learning. For too many people, learning is something that stops when they leave school. Learning new skills, at work and for pleasure, must become a rewarding part of everyday life.

- We must make colleges and training providers more responsive to employers' and learners' needs, reaching out to more businesses and more people, and providing training in ways that suit them. Creating a truly demand-led approach means reforming qualifications, reforming the way we fund colleges, and reforming the way we deliver training.

- We must achieve much better joint working across Government and the public services. This is not just a strategy for the Department for Education and Skills, but a shared strategy involving the Department of Trade and Industry, the Department for Work and Pensions, the Treasury and the range of agencies involved in training, skills, business support and productivity. Government must lead by example, in the way that we work and in our own role as employers.

12. As a Government, we have an ambitious agenda for transforming our society and economy. Much of that agenda is dependent on developing ever higher skills, in our young people, in the workforce and across the community. In preparing this Skills Strategy, we have consulted widely to identify the major obstacles and build on the many creative ideas for improvement. We welcome the commitment of many partners who have helped to shape this strategy. We will carry forward that partnership in turning the strategy into action.

Tony Blair
Prime Minister

Charles Clarke
Secretary of State for Education and Skills

Patricia Hewitt
Secretary of State for Trade and Industry

Gordon Brown
Chancellor of the Exchequer

Andrew Smith
Secretary of State for Work and Pensions

Summary of the Skills Strategy

AIM

1. The aim of this national Skills Strategy is to ensure that employers have the right skills to support the success of their businesses, and individuals have the skills they need to be both employable and personally fulfilled.

CONTEXT

2. Since 1997, the Government has developed policies based on the interdependence of social justice and economic success. Record low levels of unemployment have been achieved, with low inflation, and high investment to modernise public services. Nonetheless, our economic productivity and competitiveness remain well below those of major competitor nations. One reason is that there are some serious gaps in our national skills base.

3. The global economy has made largely extinct the notion of a 'job for life'. The imperative now is employability for life. Competing on the basis of low wage costs is not an option. We must compete on the basis of our capability for innovation, enterprise, quality, and adding greater value through our products and services. All of that is dependent on raising our skills game.

4. Over the past six years we have made major progress. From Sure Start and universal nursery provision through to higher education, we have developed a reform agenda to raise standards for children and young people throughout their initial education. These reforms, coupled with record investment, will deliver a future flow of higher skilled, better qualified young people into the labour market.

5. We have also worked to raise skill levels amongst adults already in the workforce. The Learning and Skills Council is bringing a new coherence to the strategic planning and funding of adult learning across colleges and work-based training. Regional Development Agencies are focusing on knowledge and skills as key drivers of economic regeneration.

THE CHALLENGE

6. Despite these real improvements, our skill gaps remains stubbornly persistent. Output per hour worked is around 25 per cent higher in the US and Germany and over 30 per cent higher in France than in the UK. While we compare well at higher education level, our percentage of the workforce qualified to intermediate skill levels (apprenticeship, skilled craft and technician level) is low: 28 per cent in the UK compared with 51 per cent in France and 65 per cent in Germany.

7. The recent Treasury assessment of the five economic tests for UK membership of the European single currency noted that a highly educated workforce with a culture of lifelong learning is more likely to adapt to economic change.[1] Improving the level of skills, particularly among those with the lowest skill levels, is a focus of the Government's agenda for enhancing flexibility in the UK.

8. We have particular skill gaps in basic skills for employability, including literacy, numeracy and use of IT; intermediate skills at apprenticeship, technician, higher craft and associate professional level; mathematics; and management and leadership. Employers have long been concerned that they are not getting recruits with the skills they want.

9. So we must do more. In developing this strategy, we have listened carefully to the concerns of employers, trade unions, colleges and other partners. They have challenged us to create a coherent policy framework focused on the needs of employers and learners. We need to mobilise the full commitment of Government, its agencies, education and training providers, employers, unions and individual learners. Isolated endeavours will not be enough.

10. The strategy is not predominantly about new initiatives. It is about making more sense of what is already there, integrating what already exists and focusing it more effectively. Our overriding goal is to ensure that everyone has the skills they need to become more employable and adaptable.

---

1   HM Treasury (2003) *UK Membership of the Single Currency: An assessment of the five economic tests*

WHAT WILL WE DO TO HELP EMPLOYERS AND LEARNERS?

11. We will work with **employers and employees** to:

    a. Give employers greater choice and control over the publicly-funded training they receive and how it is delivered. Evaluation of the current Employer Training Pilots will inform the development of future national programmes to support skills training.

    b. Provide better information for employers about the quality of local training by introducing an *Employer Guide to Good Training*.

    c. Improve training and development for management and leadership, particularly in small firms centred around the new Investors in People management and leadership model.

    d. Develop business support services to ensure that employers have better access to the advice and help they want, from the sources best placed to provide it, bringing in a wider range of intermediaries.

    e. Expand and strengthen the network of Union Learning Representatives as a key plank in encouraging the low skilled to engage in training.

12. For **individual learners**, we will:

    a. Create a new guarantee of free tuition for any adult without a good foundation of employability skills to get the training they need to achieve such a qualification (known as a 'level 2' qualification).

    b. Increase support for higher level skills at technician, higher craft or associate professional level (known as a 'level 3' qualification), in areas of sectoral or regional skill priority.

    c. Pilot a new form of adult learning grant, providing weekly financial support for adults studying full-time for their first full level 2 qualification, and for young adults studying for their first full level 3 qualification.

    d. Safeguard the provision in each local area of a wide range of learning for adults, for culture, leisure, community and personal fulfilment purposes, with a better choice of opportunities to encourage adults back into learning.

    e. Provide better information, advice and guidance on skills, training and qualifications, so that people know what is available, what the benefits are, and where to go.

    f. Help adults gain ICT skills, as a third basic skill alongside literacy and numeracy in our *Skills for Life* programme.

13. A key means of raising our game on skills is through the Sector Skills Council network. We are on track to establish 23 Councils by summer 2004. The Councils will be a major new voice for employers and employees in each major sector of the economy. We will support the development of sector skills agreements, setting a longer term agenda for raising productivity in each sector, the skills needed for international competitiveness, and how employers might work together on a voluntary basis to invest in the necessary skills.

14. The Sector Skills Councils need to be major contributors at regional as well as national level. There is a strong regional dimension to the skills problem. Variations in the skills base of the regions are a major factor in explaining regional variations in productivity. Regional Development Agencies lead in producing Frameworks for Regional Employment and Skills Action (FRESAs) designed to address the skills and employment needs of employers and individuals in the regions within an economic, demographic and social context.

HOW WILL WE BRING ABOUT THESE CHANGES?

15. To achieve these gains, we need to take concerted action to reform the supply and delivery of publicly-funded education and training.

16. We will reform the **qualifications framework** so that it is more flexible and responsive to the needs of employers and learners by:

    a. Strengthening and extending Modern Apprenticeships, as a top quality vocational route designed to meet the needs of employers. We will lift the current age cap, so that adults will be able to benefit.

    b. Reviewing, through the work of the group led by Mike Tomlinson, the vocational routes available to young people, and strengthening the focus on their employability and enterprise skills.

    c. Making qualifications for adults more flexible by dividing more learning programmes into units and speeding up accreditation of new qualifications.

    d. Introducing a credits framework for adults, to help both learners and employers package the training programmes they want, and build up a record of achievement over time towards qualifications.

    e. Making it easier for people to gain the skills they need by reviewing in each sector the need for new adult learning programmes to develop generic skills for employment.

17. We already have in place the major *Success for All* reform programme to **raise the effectiveness of further education colleges and training providers.** We will build on that by:

    a. Reforming the funding arrangements for adult learning and skills, to give training providers stronger incentives to work with employers while reducing bureaucracy. This will include introducing a new approach to setting fees and raising income.

b. Supporting the development of e-learning across further education, with more on-line learning materials and assessment.

c. Helping colleges build their capability to offer a wider range of business support for local employers.

d. Broadening the range of training providers, by bringing within the scope of public funding those private providers who have something distinctive and high quality to offer.

18. We recognise that Government must lead by example, showing that **we and our delivery agencies can work more effectively together at national, regional and local level** in providing coherent services for skills, business support and the labour market. We will:

a. Form a national Skills Alliance, bringing together the key Government departments with employer and union representatives as a new social partnership, and linking the key delivery agencies in a concerted drive to raise skills.

b. Link implementation of the Skills Strategy with the conclusions of the Department of Trade and Industry Innovation Review, so that both skills and innovation work together as two key drivers enhancing productivity.

c. Integrate the work of Regional Development Agencies, the Sector Skills Council network, the Small Business Service, the Learning and Skills Council and Jobcentre Plus, inviting the Regional Development Agency in each region to develop innovative proposals for effective collaboration. The focus will be on simplifying the system for employers and learners, improving value for money, raising aspirations and responding to local and regional skills needs.

d. Strengthen the partnership between the Learning and Skills Council and Jobcentre Plus, with a stronger push to support skills and training for benefit claimants, and provide a better integrated service for employers.

e. Build up education and training opportunities for offenders through closer working between the Prison Service, the Probation Service, the Learning and Skills Council, Ufi/**learndirect** and other partners.

f. As a major employer in our own right, the Government will invest in the skills of our staff to achieve our public service objectives.

Chapter 1

Overview: The Skills Challenge and How We Will Meet It

AIM AND VISION

1.1 This strategy seeks to ensure that, across the nation, employers have the right skills to support the success of their businesses and organisations, and individuals have the skills they need to be both employable and personally fulfilled.

1.2 We aim to:

    a. Improve the UK's productivity and standard of living. That will contribute to the Government's central economic objective of raising the rate of sustainable growth across all English regions, to achieve rising prosperity and a better quality of life, with economic and employment opportunities for all. It will also support our wider efforts to encourage economic reform in Europe.

    b. Build a better society by helping people gain the skills to work productively in the private, public and voluntary sectors, supplying the goods and services people want.

    c. Help individuals acquire and keep developing the skills to support sustained employability, more rewarding lives, and a greater contribution to their communities.

1.3 A better skilled workforce is a more productive workforce. We must improve our productivity, and our ability to support sustainable development, if we are to compete successfully in today's global market. Improving skills will not be sufficient on its own to drive greater productivity. But taken together with enterprise, competition, investment and innovation, it has a crucial role to play.

1.4 Government cannot do this alone. We need to build a new Skills Alliance, where every employer, every employee and every citizen plays their part. No business should be left behind because it lacks the opportunity to improve the knowledge and skills of its staff. No individual should be denied the chance to realise their potential for want of opportunities to invest in their own skills.

1.5 This is not only an economic challenge. It is just as much a social one. By increasing the skill levels of all under-represented groups, we will develop an inclusive society that promotes employability for all. When people are better educated and better trained, they have the chance to earn more and use their talents to the full, both in and out of work. They are better able to use their skills for the benefit of their families and their communities. There is strong evidence to suggest that improving skill levels can reduce the risk of unemployment, and bring broader social returns in terms of reduced crime and better health.

WHY DO WE NEED A SKILLS STRATEGY?

1.6 We have many strengths in the way we develop skills, learning and qualifications in this country. Thanks to recent school reforms, our young people compare well internationally in their literacy, numeracy and science skills.[2] We are as good at developing highly skilled graduates as the best in the world.[3] Our universities have greatly improved the spin-out benefits from their research, in supporting innovation and new product and company development. There is a rich range of opportunities for adult learning. We have a highly flexible labour market, and low levels of unemployment.

1.7 But despite these strengths, the way we develop skills and their contribution to productivity remains a serious weakness. French, German and US workers produce between a quarter and a third more in every hour they work than their British counterparts.[4] Output per worker is 16 per cent higher in France, and 31 per cent higher in the US.[5] The recent Treasury assessment of the five economic tests for UK membership of the European single currency noted that a highly educated workforce with a culture of lifelong learning is more likely to adapt to economic change. Improving the level of skills, particularly among those with the lowest skill levels, is a focus of the Government's agenda for enhancing flexibility in the UK. Inside

---

2 OECD (2002) *Programme for International Student Assessment, Reading for Change*, OECD
3 OECD (2002) *Education at a Glance*, OECD
4 Office for National Statistics, (2003) *International Comparisons of Productivity*
5 HM Treasury (2003) *Budget report*. US skills levels may be substantially understated by the conventional data, due to the lack of nationally recognised qualifications. Some studies classify US high school graduates as low-skilled. This is true of some, but others receive high quality vocational and general training. US data rarely include workplace training, cited by over 35 per cent of US workers as a significant source of skills.

or outside the European Monetary Union, but particularly within a single currency area, individuals need the skills to adapt to increased competition and to compete for a wide range of jobs in a changing economic environment.[6] Table 1 summarises the key skills gaps.

Table 1 Labour force skills, total economy, 1999				
	Percentage of the workforce with qualifications at levels:			Relative skills
	Higher	Intermediate	Low	UK=100
US	27.7	18.6	53.7	100.5
France	16.4	51.2	32.4	105.5
Germany	15.0	65.0	20.0	105.3
UK	15.4	27.7	56.9	100

Source: O'Mahony and De Boer (2002) *Britain's relative productivity performance: update and extensions*, NIESR

1.8 In March 2003 we published an analysis of the nature of our skills challenge.[7] The key problems we identified were that:

a. Employers feel they are not getting recruits with the right skills.

b. We have particular skills gaps in:

   i. Basic skills (including literacy, language, numeracy and computer skills) which provide the foundation for further learning.

   ii. The percentage of the workforce with intermediate skills (associate professional, apprenticeship, technician, or skilled craft or trade level).

   iii. Mathematics – which is an essential basis for further technical training.

   iv. Leadership and management skills.

c. There is too often a mismatch between what employers and individuals want, and the courses and qualifications available through publicly-funded colleges and training providers.[8]

d. Equally, many private and public sector organisations undervalue how a better skilled, trained and qualified workforce can improve their 'bottom line' performance. Such organisations can experience a 'low skills equilibrium', producing low value-added products and services, making it harder for us to compete internationally.

6   HM Treasury (2003) *UK Membership of the Single Currency: An assessment of the five economic tests*
7   Department for Education and Skills (2003) *Developing a National Skills Strategy and Delivery Plan: underlying evidence*
8   The term 'colleges and training providers' refers to colleges, work-based learning providers, specialist providers, employers and others delivering learning funded by the Learning and Skills Council (LSC) for England

e.   Many individuals do not see how better skills, training and qualifications can help them achieve their personal goals, whether for financial rewards through better jobs and higher wages, for supporting their families and communities, or for their own personal fulfilment. We are concerned that skills and learning initiatives are not reaching all of society. We want to increase the skill levels for all under-represented groups and encourage all individuals to improve their employability. This is crucial for women workers who now constitute 44 per cent of the workforce, yet are typically locked in a narrow range of low level manual occupations and in part-time work where training opportunities are limited. It is also an issue for ethnic minorities, agency workers and other disadvantaged groups who have low skill levels. Lack of investment in training can restrict their career options and ability to achieve rewarding, stable jobs.

f.   Many believe that the Government and its agencies do not approach skills and productivity issues coherently. That makes it difficult for employers and learners to understand what support is available and how to access it.

g.   The respective roles and responsibilities of Government, employers and individuals in terms of paying for and organising training and qualifications remain unclear.

HOW WILL WE TACKLE THIS CHALLENGE?

1.9   The Skills Strategy aims to address these deep-rooted and pervasive problems. During the course of the past six years, significant progress has been made in our quest to make high quality lifelong learning a reality from the cradle to the grave. Annex 1 draws together the main strands:

a.   In schools, our literacy and numeracy programmes have achieved real improvements in pupil performance.

b.   At GCSE and A level, exam results have risen significantly.

c.   Our specialist schools programme, and curriculum and examination reforms, have increased the emphasis on equipping pupils with the skills, knowledge and understanding they need for employability.

d.   In higher education, there has been a major expansion in student places. We have introduced Foundation Degrees as a new vocational option. We have encouraged universities to work closely with business and employers.

e.   In further education, student numbers have increased. We are reforming the quality and responsiveness of colleges and training providers. We have established the Learning and Skills Council as a powerful new body for planning and allocating over £8 billion which the state spends each year on post-16 education and training.

f. Our *Skills for Life*[9] programme is tackling poor levels of literacy, language and numeracy skills among adults.

1.10 All of this represents a lot of hard work by schools, colleges and universities, resulting in real improvement.

1.11 The White Paper builds on the extensive skills and adult learning reforms put in place since 1997. It addresses frequently articulated concerns of employers, trade unions and providers. They have challenged us to create a coherent policy framework which supports frontline delivery and develops an education and training system which is focused on the needs of employers and learners. Isolated individual initiatives will not be enough, since such endeavours have not had sufficient impact in the past. We need to draw together all the major partners. We need also to connect the many existing programmes and activities, so that they form a shared, sustained and determined programme for change.

1.12 So this strategy is not predominantly about new initiatives, but rather about making more sense of what is already there, integrating what already exists, and focusing it more effectively.

1.13 The key themes which characterise this strategy are:

a. **Putting employers' needs centre stage.** Skills are not an end in themselves, but a means towards supporting successful businesses and organisations. We must give employers more support in accessing the training they need, and more influence in deciding how that training is provided. This is what we mean by a 'demand-led' system.

b. **Helping employers use skills to achieve more ambitious longer term business success.** The Skills Strategy is not just about meeting the demands for skills that employers already have. We must also help those employers who want to increase productivity, to upgrade to higher value-added products and services, or to set up new, higher value businesses, to secure the higher level skills needed to achieve those ambitions. Our new sector skills agreements described in chapter 3 will be central to this.

c. **Motivating and supporting learners.** We will make it easier for those adults who most need extra skills by offering them a new entitlement to learning. We will prioritise our resources, with the ambition that over time we help everybody who wants them to gain at least the foundation skills for employability, with better support for young adults to gain more advanced craft, technician and associate professional qualifications.

---

9   Department for Education and Skills (2001) *Skills for Life* – the national strategy for improving adult literacy and numeracy skills,

d. **Enabling colleges and training providers to be more responsive to employers' and learners' needs.** Our best colleges and training providers already show abundant creativity and commitment in meeting local needs. But too often 'the system' gets in their way – the framework for planning, funding, monitoring, qualifications and student support does not give incentives or clear signals to support active, effective reach-out to meet needs.

e. **Joint Government action in a new Skills Alliance.** We will link up the work of the key Government departments involved with economic and skills issues – the Department for Education and Skills, the Department of Trade and Industry, the Department for Work and Pensions, and the Treasury. The same collaborative approach will apply at regional level, between the Regional Development Agencies, the Learning and Skills Council and their partners. We will establish a new Skills Alliance, bringing together Government departments, agencies and representatives of employers and employees, to create a new social partnership for skills.

1.14 The Skills Strategy is primarily a strategy for England, reflecting the devolution of responsibility for education and training to Scotland, Wales and Northern Ireland. Each has developed its own strategies for skills and lifelong learning.[10] However, some elements of this strategy have implications for the Devolved Administrations, notably the work of the Sector Skills Councils (which have a UK-wide remit) and the proposed sector skills agreements. The strategy has been developed in consultation with them and is consistent with the direction of their policies for skills.

WHAT WILL WE DO TO HELP EMPLOYERS AND LEARNERS?

We will strengthen the supply of skills to deliver what employers want in the way that they want it…

1.15 The best British employers are world-leaders, producing high value-added goods and services with innovative, productive and enterprising workforces. But if we are to sustain our place as a leading global economy, we need to increase the proportion of organisations focusing on high value-added, high specification products where jobs require advanced skills and training, and pay correspondingly high wages. It is not for the Government to tell private business what products and services to invest in. But it is the Government's role to offer support to businesses to increase productivity and invest in innovation, so that they stand the best chance of success. That means encouraging and helping employers to invest in skills and training in a more strategic

---

10 Scottish Executive (2003) *Life Through Learning; Learning Through Life: A Strategy for Lifelong Learning*
Welsh Assembly Government (2001) *The Learning Country;* Welsh Assembly Government (2002) *A Winning Wales: National Economic Development Strategy;* Welsh Assembly Government (2002) *Skills and Employment Action Plan for Wales*
The Department of Employment and Learning Northern Ireland published in June 2003 a strategic plan from which will flow a skills strategy for Northern Ireland to be published at the end of 2003

way, linked to business strategies, human resource strategies and product-market strategies.

1.16 **We will work with employers and employees to:**

    a. **Give businesses greater choice and control** over the content and delivery of the training they receive. Government investment in such training should particularly address areas of market failure, by supporting employers in training their low skilled workers. Evaluation of the current Employer Training Pilots, which focus on supporting training for those with low or no qualifications, will inform the development of future national programmes to support skills training.

    b. **Provide better information** for employers about the quality of local training. We will introduce an *Employer Guide to Good Training*, offering straightforward quality and performance information from each local Learning and Skills Council about local colleges and training providers. The 'business.gov' website will be developed as a prime source of on-line information and services for business.

    c. **Improve training and development for leadership and management**, particularly in small and medium sized businesses. With Investors in People, the developing network of Sector Skills Councils (known as the Skills for Business Network) and other partners, we will develop a new programme, linked to the new Investors in People Management and Leadership model.

    d. **Develop business support services** to offer employers better information about where to get help. We will strengthen the existing Business Link network so that it offers better support in linking higher skills to stronger business performance, with clearer signposting of what help is available and where to get it, bringing in a wider range of intermediaries.

    e. **Support the expanding network of Union Learning Representatives.** Unions can play an important part in raising the profile of training and skills as an investment in organisational success. Learning representatives in the workplace have proved effective in encouraging the low skilled to engage in training, as well as supporting those with higher level skills and encouraging continuous professional development.

    f. **Strengthen the Modern Apprenticeships programme** to make it more flexible, lifting the age limit so that more older learners can participate and bringing in a wider range of employers.

1.17 A key means of raising our game on skills is through the new Sector Skills Council network known as the **Skills for Business Network.** The network will be the main voice for employers and employees in each sector, identifying sector skill needs and how best to meet them. New sector skills agreements will have powerful leverage over the supply of training and skills at regional and local level. They will need to be based on excellent analysis of skills, productivity and labour market trends and gaps.

We will strengthen support for individual learners, with better information, clearer targeting of funds, and more help to return to learning…

1.18 Significantly more young people in England leave education or training by the age of 17 than in most other developed countries. The legacy of this high drop out rate is that too many adults lack minimum levels of basic and employability skills, and are not interested in further learning. They often lack the necessary support to re-engage in learning and are the least likely group to receive training from their employers. We must target funding on those areas where skill needs are the greatest, while still providing a framework which motivates and supports adults to want to engage in skills training and qualifications at all levels from basic skills to higher education.

1.19 **For individual learners, we will:**

a. **Create a new entitlement to free learning for anyone without a good foundation of employability skills to get the training they need to achieve such a qualification.** Those who do not have a qualification at level 2[11] are less likely to get secure, well paid jobs, and are more likely to suffer disadvantage and exclusion.

b. **Provide targeted support for higher level skills at technician, higher craft or associate professional level.** This support will be focused on those who are developing their skills and qualifications to level 3[12], in priority areas to meet sectoral and regional skill needs. The support will be provided through the new regional skills partnerships, and delivered by the local Learning and Skills Councils.

c. **Pilot the delivery of a new learning grant for adults in further education.** This will be modelled on the existing education maintenance allowance for 16–19 year olds. It will be aimed at adults studying full-time[13] for their first full level 2 qualification, and young adults studying full-time for their first full level 3 qualification.

d. **Safeguard the provision in each local area of a wide range of learning for adults, for culture, leisure, community and personal fulfilment purposes.** While giving priority to better work-related skills training, each local Learning and Skills Council will have a defined budget to work with others to support that range of learning, including learning for pensioners.

e. **Provide better information, advice and guidance on skills, training and qualifications, so that people know what is available, what the benefits are, and where to go.** To achieve this, we will combine the network of local advice partnerships with the national advice helpline provided by Ufi/**learndirect**.

11 A full level 2 refers to any qualification equivalent in standard and breadth to 5 GCSEs at A* -C or a National Vocational Qualification at level 2
12 A full level 3 refers to a standard equivalent to two A levels or a National Vocational Qualification at level 3
13 Full-time is a programme of at least 450 guided learning hours in a 12 month period

f. **Provide a better choice of opportunities to encourage adults back into learning.** That will draw together the network of 6,000 UK online centres, 2,000 Ufi/**learndirect** centres, and the many community, college and local authority learning programmes.

g. **Develop opportunities to gain skills in using Information and Communications Technology (ICT).** Basic ICT skills will become a third area of adult basic skills, alongside literacy and numeracy within our *Skills for Life* programme.

1.20 We believe that the new entitlement to free learning, taken with the other reforms set out in this strategy, provide many of the elements we previously sought to develop through the Individual Learning Accounts. We continue to attach importance to the principles of adults being motivated and helped to return to learning, through wider choice and a stronger sense of ownership of the funds that support their learning. We shall seek to apply those principles as we implement the strategy.

HOW WILL WE DO IT?

1.21 To meet these challenges, we need to take action across a range of fronts.

We will reform the qualifications framework, so that it is more flexible and responsive to the needs of employers and individual learners…

1.22 There is much concern that the existing range of qualifications is not providing what employers require and individuals need. More 14–19 year olds are gaining better qualifications. But the vocational route remains poorly regarded and misunderstood. A review led by the former Chief Inspector of Schools, Mike Tomlinson, is considering how to improve the vocational options for 14–19 year olds, in order to give young people in secondary schools and colleges a much firmer foundation of skills to prepare them for their working lives.

1.23 For adults, the main learning programmes and qualifications available often do not fit the bill in terms of developing a broad foundation of skills to support long term employability. So we will reform qualifications, so that they better meet the needs of employers, and lead to better rewards and employment prospects for learners:

a. **We will strengthen Modern Apprenticeships**, as a top quality vocational route. We will better integrate key skills into Modern Apprenticeship programmes, lift the age cap so that adults can also benefit from Modern Apprenticeship programmes, and involve employers more closely in promoting Modern Apprenticeships.

b. **We will review, through the work of the group led by Mike Tomlinson, the vocational routes available to young people**, and strengthen the focus on employability skills and enterprise for young people.

c. **We are developing a wide range of vocational Foundation Degree courses** in universities and colleges, so that as we expand places in higher education, we meet higher level skill needs.

d. **Qualifications for adults will be made more flexible.** The Qualifications and Curriculum Authority is working with the Learning and Skills Council and the Sector Skills Development Agency to develop proposals for greater flexibility. This includes dividing more qualifications into units; speeding up accreditation of new qualifications; and better assessment of people's existing skills and knowledge.

e. **We will develop a credit framework for adults**, to provide greater flexibility for both learners and employers in packaging the learning programmes that best suit their needs. As the first step, we will invite the bodies which award the largest number of qualifications to adults to collaborate, under the leadership of the Qualifications and Curriculum Authority, to develop a shared credit-based approach.

f. **We will make it easier for people to acquire the skills needed for employment.** We will review in each major employment sector the need for new adult learning programmes to develop generic 'skills for employment'. People might acquire a 'skills passport' or 'skills foundation' which records their key and generic skills.

We will work with colleges and training providers to help them respond more effectively in providing skills, training and qualifications to meet employer and learner needs…

1.24 Learning and Skills Council surveys show that most learners are satisfied with their courses. There has been a substantial growth in the number of learners – nearly 500,000 extra learners (a 13 per cent increase) in funded learning since 1996/97.

1.25 But standards of learning and achievement vary, and there remain problems with finding the right course at the right time. The *Success for All* programme launched in 2002 is already raising standards. We will build on that by:

a. **Reforming the funding arrangements for adult learning and skills**, to give colleges and training providers stronger incentives to work flexibly with employers while reducing bureaucracy. Within the regional framework for skills priorities, and local Learning and Skills Council plans, colleges and training providers will have more freedom to decide what training programmes to offer, and how to deliver them.

b. **Supporting the development of e-learning across the sector**, with more on-line learning materials and assessment, supported by £200 million from the Learning and Skills Council over three years.

c. **Helping colleges build their capability to offer a wider range of business support for local employers.** Many successful colleges already provide such support, including Centres of Vocational Excellence. We wish to build on their experience.

d. **Broadening the range of training providers**, by bringing within the scope of public funding those private providers who offer distinctive, high quality training and can best meet gaps in current provision.

1.26 One goal of the Skills Strategy is to clarify the roles and responsibilities of Government, learners and employers, including who should pay for what. We believe it is right in principle that those who benefit most financially should also contribute to the cost, while protecting the interests of those who need most help and cannot afford to pay. The Government should be clear about our priorities, so that we can focus public funds where they will achieve most benefit, particularly in raising national competitiveness and creating sustainable employment.

1.27 We want to encourage the development of skills right across the board. Supporting the development of higher level skills and qualifications is every bit as important in a knowledge economy as helping those with no or low skills. Many of our skills deficits are at those higher levels. So the strategy must provide a framework which encourages such investment. But that is different from deciding who pays for it. The state cannot pay for everything. So in deciding the right focus for allocating public funds, we must take account of where there are market failures which block investment in skills, as distinct from where the rates of return to individuals and their employers make it fair to expect them to contribute to the costs of their own learning.

1.28 On this basis, our priorities in using public funds are:

a. The introduction of an entitlement to free learning for adults without qualifications, to help them gain a full level 2 skills foundation for employability. This extends the existing priority of improving adults' basic skills in literacy, language and numeracy.

b. Supporting those who are developing their qualifications to a higher level in technician, advanced craft and associate professional skills, particularly where those meet sectoral and regional skills priorities.

c. Supporting those who are re-skilling for new careers, and those preparing to return to the labour market, again particularly where that meets sectoral and regional skills priorities.

d. Safeguarding a varied range of learning opportunities for personal fulfilment, community development and active citizenship.

1.29 Providing more support in these areas means re-prioritising public funds. In consequence, we believe it is fair that those learners (or their employers) who already have good qualifications and who wish to undertake further study at the same or a lower level, should pay more. There will still be substantial public funds available to meet some of the costs of their courses. The vast majority of learners will still be receiving support from public funds towards the costs of their training. But we need to balance the contributions from the state, individuals and employers so that they more fairly reflect the benefits gained. So we propose to establish a new framework for raising income and setting fees in further education, consulting on the best approach. We propose that in future, each college and training provider should agree an overall income target with the Learning and Skills Council as part of its development plan. This new element of development planning will be phased in from 2004/05. Colleges will be free to develop their own strategies for securing fee income or other revenue.

We will deliver these changes by ensuring that Government and its agencies take an effective lead, and work more closely together in supporting skills and productivity…

1.30 For these changes to happen, the Government must lead by example, showing its own determination to lead a sustained and concerted strategy. The key measures are:

a. **Our new national Skills Alliance**, bringing together the key Government departments and agencies with employer and union representatives. The Alliance will represent a new social partnership for skills between Government, the CBI, the Trades Union Congress (TUC) and the Small Business Council, working with a group of key delivery partners. It will pursue a shared agenda in raising productivity for the common good. It will be led by the Secretaries of State for Education and Skills, and Trade and Industry.

b. **We will integrate implementation of the Skills Strategy with the conclusions of the Department of Trade and Industry's Innovation Review.** Innovation cannot flourish if companies do not have the skills to create, understand and apply new knowledge in developing new and improved goods and services. Equally, skills will not be fully utilised if companies are not innovating.

c. **We will integrate the work of Regional Development Agencies, the Skills for Business Network, the Small Business Service, the local Learning and Skills Councils, and Jobcentre Plus.** This will mean that in each region there is a strong connection between the skills needed to raise productivity by region and sector, and the allocation of funds to training providers. Regional Development Agencies will lead discussions with partners in each region to develop proposals for a regional skills partnership accountable for setting priorities and driving action on skills and productivity. These will build on existing networks supporting the Framework for Regional Employment and Skills Action (FRESA).

d. **We will develop a stronger link between the Department for Education and Skills and the Department for Work and Pensions**, and between the operations of Jobcentre Plus and the national Learning and Skills Council. We will give more encouragement for benefit claimants (including those on long term inactive benefits) to gain skills and qualifications to boost their chances of good jobs, and will review ways to give priority to placing people in jobs with training. We want stronger joint working at local level between Jobcentre Plus and the Learning and Skills Council, and will build this into the proposals for the regional skills partnership.

e. **We will support the development of learning communities**. We will ask the Government Office in each region to support Regional Development Agencies, local Learning and Skills Councils and Local Strategic Partnerships in their region to identify suitable areas.

f. **We will build up education and training opportunities in prisons** through closer working between the Prison Service, the Probation Service, the Learning and Skills Council, Ufi/**learndirect** and other partners, so that ex-offenders have a better prospect of getting secure employment and avoiding re-offending.

1.31 The Government will lead by example as a major employer in its own right, to ensure that all Government departments are investing in the skills needed for their sectors. That will help achieve our objectives for public service reform.

WHAT WOULD SUCCESS LOOK LIKE?

1.32 The Skills Strategy will only work if it brings benefits to employers and learners. The real measure of success is whether individual employers and learners see a difference. The two tables at annex 2 summarise our aspirations for the differences we hope individual employers and learners would in time see, set against the main measures set out in detail in subsequent chapters which would secure that difference.

RIGHTS AND RESPONSIBILITIES

1.33 A successful strategy will bring enormous economic and social benefits to the nation, employers and individual learners. But that is not to say that everyone will get what they want, or that change will be easy. There are some hard decisions that have to be taken, striking a balance between the interests and preferences of different groups. As noted in paragraphs 1.26 to 1.29 above, this applies particularly in deciding who should pay for what.

1.34 The 2001 Budget report set out the Government's belief that, although voluntary approaches have secured increased participation in workplace training, they have not been sufficient given the scale of the problem. Addressing this problem is a priority and will require a step-change on the part of employers, individuals and the Government. The Government is therefore seeking to develop policies through this strategy which will help employers and individuals to meet their responsibilities in this area.

1.35 The main rights and responsibilities are set out in table 2 below.

Table 2: Rights and responsibilities	
Employers	Employers have the right to expect that: ● The public service of education and training will be responsive to their needs in providing skills to meet current and future demands ● Training, skills and qualifications will be provided within a context that supports productivity, innovation and wider business performance, rather than promoted as ends in themselves ● Education must equip young people with the skills, knowledge and competences employers need ● Skills, training and qualifications will be high quality, responsive and up-to-date ● Public funds should be available, within budget constraints, to support the wider goals of learning, to promote generic skills and long term employability, going beyond employers' own needs In return, employers have responsibilities to invest in training, and to use the skills and competences gained, so as to achieve the gains in productivity and organisational performance necessary to secure international competitiveness and high quality public services. Where appropriate, employers should work in partnership with recognised unions and their Union Learning Representatives to develop a workplace learning culture and to tackle low skills. Employers already invest very large sums in staff training, and that will need to be sustained, reflecting the benefits to employers of a highly skilled workforce. Employers rightly focus on the success of their own organisation. They are accountable to shareholders, owners and directors for securing and exploiting the skills required to achieve organisational goals. But no business operates in isolation. In a highly inter-connected and inter-dependent world, the Government also has a role to promote long term, as well as short term, gains from skills, and the value of broad-based training programmes and qualifications in promoting wider employability and labour market flexibility. The Government will also encourage involvement on the part of employers in helping training providers understand their skill needs and provide work-based experience for young people. Employers can be powerful advocates for skills. We have a network of champions for adult basic skills, and want to extend that approach.

Individuals	Individuals have the right to expect that:

- The public service of education and training will be responsive to their needs as actual or potential learners
- Education and training will be delivered to a high standard
- Courses and qualifications will be relevant and up-to-date, leading to higher rewards and better employment prospects in the labour market

Low skilled adults will be entitled to more support than in the past, to help all achieve a skills foundation for employability.

In return, some learners – and particularly those who already have higher level qualifications seeking further qualifications at the same or lower level – are likely to need to contribute more to the costs, recognising the substantial benefits that accrue to higher levels of qualification. There is also a responsibility for individuals to contribute to the success of the organisation that employs them by discussing their skill needs with their employer and participating in training programmes tailored to the needs of the organisation.

Providers	Publicly-funded training providers have the right to expect the Government to set a regulatory and funding framework for training and skills which:

- Is clear, equitable and consistent
- Gives them maximum discretion to run their own operations and take their own decisions in matters they are best placed to judge
- Encourages innovation and creativity
- Imposes the minimum of bureaucracy consistent with accountability

In return, providers are responsible for delivering training programmes which are higher quality and more responsive than in the past to the needs of employers and learners in terms of content and delivery.

1.36 Our aim is to establish an effective infrastructure to support the delivery of these roles and responsibilities. Chapter 7 sets out in detail the role of regional and local partnerships and the specific contributions of different agencies. Chart 1 below summarises the approach we propose.

Chart 1

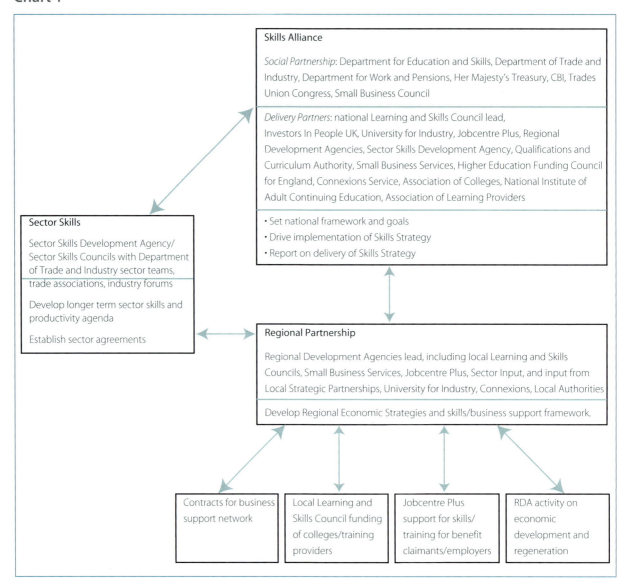

Skills Alliance

Social Partnership: Department for Education and Skills, Department of Trade and Industry, Department for Work and Pensions, Her Majesty's Treasury, CBI, Trades Union Congress, Small Business Council

Delivery Partners: national Learning and Skills Council lead, Investors In People UK, University for Industry, Jobcentre Plus, Regional Development Agencies, Sector Skills Development Agency, Qualifications and Curriculum Authority, Small Business Services, Higher Education Funding Council for England, Connexions Service, Association of Colleges, National Institute of Adult Continuing Education, Association of Learning Providers

- Set national framework and goals
- Drive implementation of Skills Strategy
- Report on delivery of Skills Strategy

Sector Skills

Sector Skills Development Agency/ Sector Skills Councils with Department of Trade and Industry sector teams, trade associations, industry forums

Develop longer term sector skills and productivity agenda

Establish sector agreements

Regional Partnership

Regional Development Agencies lead, including local Learning and Skills Councils, Small Business Services, Jobcentre Plus, Sector Input, and input from Local Strategic Partnerships, University for Industry, Connexions, Local Authorities

Develop Regional Economic Strategies and skills/business support framework.

Contracts for business support network

Local Learning and Skills Council funding of colleges/training providers

Jobcentre Plus support for skills/ training for benefit claimants/employers

RDA activity on economic development and regeneration

DELIVERING THE STRATEGY

1.37 Achieving our objectives is a long term goal. It will require sustained commitment over many years. Chapter 8 sets out our delivery plan, in terms of priorities and timescales.

1.38 The strategy reflects widespread discussion and consultation with many parties. In autumn 2002, we hosted a series of regional skills roadshows. In March 2003, we issued an interim progress report and evidence paper for consultation. There have been seminars and discussions with a wide range of stakeholders to consider specific issues, including discussions organised by the Learning and Skills Council as part of the 'great skills debate'. We are very grateful to all those who have contributed. The strategy attempts to reflect the full range of views and discussion. A summary of the written responses to the consultation is being published separately on our website at www.dfes.gov.uk/skillsstrategy. Also available at www.dfes.gov.uk/ria is the regulatory impact assessment.

1.39 We intend to press ahead rapidly with implementing the strategy. But we welcome further comments and views. If you would like to comment, please complete the form at annex 5 and return to the address below by 31 October 2003.

Consultation Unit
Department for Education and Skills
Area 1B
Castle View House
East Lane
Runcorn
Cheshire
WA7 2GJ

or by email to SkillsStrategy.comments@dfes.gsi.gov.uk

Chapter 2

Skills for Employers, Support for Employees

SUMMARY OF THIS CHAPTER

2.1   In England alone employers spend an estimated £23 billion each year on training-related activities.[14] Many have an outstanding record in delivering added-value through innovation and sustained investment in the training and development of their people. We need to build on this commitment so that more employers place skills investment within their longer term business strategies to help improve their business performance.

2.2   But we recognise this is a two-way process. The Government must do more to support employers by focusing on the needs of employers and employees as the customers. Small, medium and larger businesses and organisations will require different levels of support. But all require training which is easily accessible, flexible in meeting their needs, integrated with other business support services, and transparent in terms of the Government contribution towards financial costs.

2.3   Many of the reforms set out in later chapters are designed to meet the needs and concerns of employers. But this chapter focuses on providing tailored solutions for employers to meet their needs and encourage more sustainable and better managed

14 Spilsbury, D (2001) *Learning and Training at Work 2000*, Department for Education and Skills Research Report 269

business strategies. In chapter 3 we set out how we will give a stronger voice to employers through a new focus on sector skills.

2.4 We will:

- **Give businesses greater choice in, and control over, their training.**

- **Improve leadership and management capability**, building on the success of Investors in People and encouraging the spread of best practice through benchmarking and the use of diagnostic tools.

- **Develop a more accessible, coherent and integrated business support network.** The network will be focused on working with businesses to meet their current and future skill needs, so that employers can more easily get sound advice on moving up the value-chain, improving the skills of their workforce to develop business performance.

- **Provide better information** for employers, particularly about the quality of training.

- **Reform Modern Apprenticeships.** Modern Apprenticeships are a key means of helping employers secure the higher level skills they need, with a strong emphasis on work-based learning. As detailed in chapter 5, we will strengthen the Modern Apprenticeship programme, to make the integration of key skills more flexible, lift the age limit, and bring in a wider range of employers.

GREATER CHOICE AND HIGHER DEMAND FOR WORKFORCE TRAINING

2.5 A demand-led approach to developing skills in the labour force must enable individual employers to access training provision in a way which meets their business needs. It must also encourage them to invest in skills and qualifications, particularly for low skilled employees. Employer Training Pilots were introduced by the Government in September last year in six local Learning and Skills Council (LSC) areas to increase the demand for training by reducing the barriers which prevent people – particularly those with lower skills – from training. They have been extended to run for two years and to cover a further six local LSC areas.

2.6 The pilots explore the impact on demand for training up to level 2 of providing a package of support which includes:

- Free training programmes.

- Support for employers to meet the costs of giving staff paid time off to train.

- Help to broker the sourcing of training, and ensure that training is provided in the way that suits the needs of learners and employers.

- Information and advice for learners and employers, including identifying their skill needs.

2.7 The pilots seek to address the market failures which are inhibiting take up of training by those with few or no qualifications, helping low skilled employees to attain level 2 skills which will increase their productivity in the workplace and establish a platform for further progression. At the same time, the pilots are giving employers more choice and control over training. Progress during the first year of the pilots has been promising. Over 2,000 employers and 10,000 learners are participating in the pilots, with a high proportion from firms employing fewer than 50 workers. Almost all learners are completing their courses successfully, and both businesses and individuals are enthusiastic about the benefits of the training they are receiving.

2.8 We are learning important lessons from the pilots about the key factors motivating employers and learners to engage in training, and the best ways to adapt training provision to the needs and pressures of the workplace. For example, the pilots have spurred more colleges and training providers to deliver training on employers' premises, at a time and in a manner suited to their shift patterns. They have encouraged tailoring of training to meet only the skills gaps identified in initial needs assessments. We are taking these lessons on board in planning for the second year of the Employer Training Pilots, and for their extension to six further LSC areas.

2.9 This extension will allow the Government to test the impact of elements within the model more thoroughly. Pilot areas will be able to explore further ways of increasing the capacity of local training providers and engaging employers in the scheme. It is important that we do not prejudge the results of the evaluation, which will complement work in other areas to inform the development of national policy. We will draw on the lessons learnt from the pilots, including the benefits of a demand-led approach, in deciding the form of any national programme to support employer training.

SUPPORT FOR LARGER EMPLOYERS

2.10 There is a stronger expectation that larger organisations will pay for the training of their staff, particularly where it is customised to meet their higher skills needs. Such employers are also more likely to have their own networks and contacts through which they can pursue their skills and business support needs.

2.11 But there are steps we can take to help larger employers improve workforce skills:

a. The Department of Trade and Industry (DTI) Innovation Review and Business Support Transformation Programme are focusing on providing more effective support for medium and larger companies. We will continue to encourage the transfer of new ideas from universities and colleges to business, including the creation of 20 new Knowledge Exchanges (as set out in the Higher Education White Paper, *The Future of Higher Education*) to help businesses make the most of new innovations.

b. The Skills for Business Network – the network of Sector Skills Councils – will provide a new network for employers of all sizes to secure the skills they need, and to encourage all employers within a sector to work together to improve training and productivity. We expect that large employers will play a key role in developing the sector skills agreements described in chapter 3.

c. Large organisations will benefit from other reforms in this strategy including a more flexible, unitised qualifications system; greater responsiveness by colleges and training providers; greater accreditation for existing skills; scrapping funding rules for training dedicated to a single employer; the establishment of Foundation Degrees; and reforms to Modern Apprenticeships.

d. Through the increase in the Union Learning Fund, announced in the 2003 Budget, we will build the positive contribution that Union Learning Representatives can make in helping employers identify skill needs and ways of meeting them, as well as providing information, advice and guidance to employees.

Case study 1: Tyne Maritime Cluster

The Tyne Maritime Cluster is an example of businesses along the supply chain working together. Shipbuilding businesses in the cluster make the best use of all available skilled labour and shipyard capacity by pooling the skills of employees or sharing work among competing suppliers. For instance, if 30 boilermakers are needed for a project, skilled workers may move from one shipyard to another to carry out the work. Alternatively, work can be moved to another yard so that an order can be met. The Sector Skills Council – the Science, Engineering and Manufacturing Technologies Alliance (SEMTA) – is working with key employers, the Regional Development Agency One North East, and the LSC to extend this arrangement so as to bring in the whole of the region. The group is chaired by the GMB Union, which has been a major driver in the cluster's development.

2.12 We welcome the offer from the CBI to lead a project – working with the Department for Education and Skills (DfES) – to identify how best to enhance skills and innovation within supply chains and clusters. This research project will produce a report in summer 2004 recommending how to spread good practice further, including proposals on funding and on a range of options for raising performance through skills and innovation.

2.13 Through the LSC's National Contracting Service, and through local LSCs, we will support those large employers who are willing to open up their existing training facilities and programmes to train more people than they need for their own purposes.

IMPROVING LEADERSHIP AND MANAGEMENT

2.14 Effective leadership and management are key to the development of competitive businesses and high quality public services. Good leaders and managers recognise the importance of workforce skills development as a fundamental building block of high performance.

2.15 Around 4.5 million people in the UK have significant management responsibilities but fewer than a quarter of these hold a management related qualification. Reports continue to show deficiencies in the level of management skills,[15] and that these are most likely to be evident in lower and middle management.[16] A range of organisations already support improved leadership and management capability. For example, the Institute of Leadership and Management supports training of over 60,000 people a year, and Ufi/**learndirect** provides a wide range of training programmes and support for management and leadership, particularly through its Premier Business Centre network.

2.16 Current initiatives to improve leadership and management include:

   a. The Chartered Management Institute last year launched a new designation of 'Chartered Manager' status for managers meeting certain criteria.[17]

   b. The Management Standards Centre[18] is developing new world class occupational standards for leadership and management by early 2004. These will underpin management learning and qualifications at all levels, act as a competence benchmark, and be a UK resource for employers and learning institutions.

   c. For the technology-driven sector, new initiatives such as New Technology Institutes and Knowledge Exchanges aim to speed the adoption of modern management practices by improving technology transfer and making links between companies in the same cluster or industry.

2.17 The Investors in People leadership and management model helps organisations assess leadership and management capacity in more depth. Working with Investors in People UK, the Sector Skills Development Agency (SSDA), the Chartered Management Institute and Ufi/**learndirect**, we will introduce a programme offering tailored support for leadership and management development in small and medium sized enterprises. The aim will be to provide mentors and coaches who can help managers develop a programme for improving their leadership and management skills, including through informal learning. The programme will give support for applying the new Investors in People model to assess leadership and management across the business.

---

15 The Council for Excellence in Leadership and Management (2002) *Managers and leaders: raising our game*; CBI (2003) *A results overview of the Regional Survey of UK Economic Trends*

16 Porter, M (2003) *UK Competitiveness: Moving to the Next Stage*

17 See www.managers.org.uk for further information on Chartered Manager status

18 See www.management-standards.org.uk for information about the Management Standards review

2.18 We expect to build on the £30 million Small Firms Initiative already being successfully implemented to encourage small firms to pursue Investors in People status. Other key Investors in People initiatives that contribute to improving leadership and management include the Profile Tool (to help organisations benchmark performance) and the Investors in People UK Ambassadors programme for outstanding employers. These will be supplemented by a new DTI-led 'inspired leadership index' and toolkit available during 2004.

INVESTORS IN PEOPLE: DEVELOPING THE STANDARD

2.19 The Investors in People standard has been a major success story since its introduction in 1991. Nearly 28,000 organisations have achieved Investors in People recognition, employing nearly one-third of the workforce in England, and a further 16,000 are committed to working towards the standard. New national targets for Investors in People recognitions and commitments will make sure that we sustain and build on the success of the standard. The targets are that by 2007, we will seek to ensure that 45 per cent of the workforce is employed by organisations that have achieved, or are working towards Investors in People; and that at least 40,000 small firms have achieved or are working towards Investors in People status.

2.20 We will develop the framework to encourage organisations to invest in their staff. Investors in People UK will develop a benchmarking programme to allow organisations to assess themselves against a profile of excellence. It will also add to its range of models to support organisations that want to develop specific aspects of their people management as part of their commitment to be recognised or re-recognised as Investors in People. Models on leadership and management, work-life balance, and staff recruitment are already available.

IMPROVING THE SUPPORT NETWORKS FOR SMALL BUSINESSES

2.21 In order to build successful organisations, and make the most of the opportunities available to them, employers need good business information, advice and support. That must be provided in a way which is meaningful to them and fits their business needs. The Business Link network, managed by the Small Business Service (SBS), is one of the main ways that the Government provides advice and support for business. We want Business Link to broaden its appeal for those businesses that do not know where to go for help, so that it can become the prime access route for small businesses seeking Government-supported services, especially support and advice on skills and business development. This will operate alongside the wide range of existing business support services provided commercially by the private sector.

2.22 Business Link is not the only organisation that provides support and advice to employers. Our aim is to build and improve the Business Link brand and network so that it will be more attractive to businesses seeking help to take advantage of a new business development opportunity, or to tackle a business challenge. Through this route, they should be able to find the best available package of business support (information, advice, funding and training) that is available from the public, private and voluntary sectors to help them start and grow. Building on the contribution of the Small Business Council (SBC) during our consultations, we intend to reform the current arrangements so that they place greater emphasis on involving and working with a wide range of intermediaries, so that businesses can get information and support from trusted business intermediaries with whom they already work.

Case study 2: The Skills Station

Hereford and Worcester LSC is currently piloting a single point of contact for advice on training and skills backed by a quality assured consortium of training providers who can provide tailored training packages for employers. In addition, employers are offered the support of Business Link to help address other business problems, and Jobcentre Plus to help with their recruitment needs. This is a 'one stop service' aimed at meeting employer needs with a minimum of bureaucracy or duplication of services.

2.23 We recognise that improvements are needed to ensure a consistently high quality of Business Link service across the country. The SBS is working to achieve this, switching the emphasis of Business Link from direct delivery of services to brokerage of a much wider range of support, and acting to ensure that demanding service targets are set and achieved by Business Link operators. If these performance improvements continue, the Business Link access brand will play a central role in brokering business support services in each region. By this route, we want to ensure that small businesses are not faced with an array of competing and conflicting offers of advice and support from different parts of Government, because in future those various services will be offered in a co-ordinated way.

2.24 The recent Government review of services for small business identified the range of providers offering support and advice to employers. Business Link, or other brokers contracted to provide expert advice, will work closely with those who are in regular touch with individual businesses, including banks, accountants, legal advisers and employer cluster groups such as Group Training Associations. This will ensure that customers are referred to Business Link, when appropriate, and from Business Link to their services. In this way, every employer should be confident they can easily and reliably access what information they need. Instead of being sent from one agency to another before getting basic advice, there will be 'no wrong door' to accessing the support they need.

2.25 To make this approach work, business support services must be better co-ordinated and delivered. In the North West, East Midlands and West Midlands regions, the Regional Development Agencies (RDAs) are managing the Business Link contract for their regions as part of a new pilot programme. This ensures that the Business Link activities are integrated within wider regional business support services. Different approaches to improving co-ordination are being tested in other regions as well. Drawing on that experience, we will introduce in each region joint arrangements to co-ordinate skills and business support services, through the regional skills partnerships discussed in chapter 7. These will bring together the SBS, RDA, local LSCs, and Jobcentre Plus.

WORKING WITH INTERMEDIARIES

2.26 One way of improving business support services is by connecting to a wider range of intermediaries who are in regular touch with businesses, including banks, accountants, legal advisers and employer cluster groups. Intermediaries play an important role in the Investors in People Small Firms Initiative (see paragraph 2.18). We would like to expand the role of intermediaries so that they help businesses recognise the benefits of training as part of business development, and know where to refer them for in-depth support. Working with Investors in People UK and other partners, we will explore with other business intermediaries how similar arrangements could work to everyone's benefit.

2.27 The Small Business Training Initiative, announced by the Chancellor in the 2003 Budget, is an example of major banks working to support small businesses through signposting them to support for training. As part of providing business advice to clients, the banks already discuss training and development with small businesses. The project aims to develop more effective ways in which banks can use this existing relationship to direct business customers, through Business Link, to those best placed to assess and help meet skills, training and employee development needs.

2.28 The SBC has established an Accountants Group which includes representatives of the Association of Chartered Certified Accountants and the Institute of Chartered Accountants. The purpose is to tackle the problems that small businesses face identifying sources of finance, and ensuring their applications are successful. Over time, this will help to build greater confidence in Business Link by accountants, leading to greater referral of small businesses to the Business Link service. The LSC is also working with banks, sector and trade organisations to use their networks and engage small firms in business, skills and management development.

2.29 The Business Investment Tool for Entrepreneurs (BITE), which is a self-assessment questionnaire for small and medium sized enterprises developed by the Council for Excellence in Management and Leadership, will be made more widely available for intermediaries. It can be a useful first step in helping businesses work out their priorities and skills needs. Intermediaries will also be able to use the standard developed by the Small Firms Enterprise Development Initiative to offer their clients an independent assessment of the business advice they offer.

BETTER INFORMATION FOR EMPLOYERS

2.30 Employers often ask for better information about the quality of training available locally. While there is plenty of information available, it is not brought together in a way that is clear and easy to understand. Each local LSC will publish an *Employer Guide to Good Training*, which will offer simple information on the quality of local learning providers, using factual information drawn from the National Register of Providers already under development. This guide will bring together data on services funded, inspection results from the Office for Standards in Education (Ofsted) and the Adult Learning Inspectorate, and information about Centres of Vocational Excellence and Beacon status.

2.31 Employers, employees and advisers (including Union Learning Representatives) will also benefit from the reforms discussed in chapter 4 on improving information, advice and guidance (IAG) for adult learners. There is much more we can do to bring together the existing national information services provided by Ufi/**learndirect** and Worktrain with local IAG provision, so that linked information about job opportunities, training opportunities, and labour market trends is readily available.

2.32 Companies can do more to improve the available information on skills and training by reporting on their own investment and its contribution to the success of their business. An independent task force, sponsored by the DTI, is looking at how companies measure and report on their human capital management, including the investment they make in their employees' knowledge and skills. The report, due this autumn, will provide guidance on best practice to help organisations measure and evaluate their workforce as a business asset.

2.33 We will develop the business.gov website, managed by the SBS, so that it becomes the key internet portal through which on-line information, advice and support services can be made available to businesses. We expect to launch the website in 2004.

STRENGTHENING THE SKILLS AND TRAINING ROLE OF TRADE UNIONS

2.34 Raising productivity through investment in skills benefits both employers and employees. Done in the right way, it will lead to greater organisational success and more rewarding jobs. So there is a strong common interest for employers and employees to collaborate in promoting skills, training and qualifications. We want to encourage employers and unions to work together in deciding how best to raise skills. We will jointly encourage this through the DTI Partnership Fund and the DfES Union Learning Fund. Currently the Partnership and Union Learning Funds overlap in providing support for activity in workplaces to support skills development and partnership, so we shall consider how best to align them. Trade unions should demonstrate their commitment to training and lifelong learning by providing relevant accredited training for their Union Learning Representatives, supporting and guiding their Learning Representatives, and working in partnership with employers to help develop a workplace culture and to tackle low skills. Investors in People UK is also working with the Trades Union Congress (TUC) to extend Investors in People through the union route.

2.35   We have ensured trade union representation on the boards of the public bodies involved in training, such as the LSC. We are committed to trade union involvement in the new Skills for Business Network, because the sector agenda for skills and productivity concerns employees just as much as employers. We will ensure that there is union representation on their boards as each new Sector Skills Council comes into operation, and will expect union involvement in Councils' subsequent work to develop sector skills agreements.

2.36   The TUC and trade unions have a vital role in encouraging individuals back into learning through help and support in the workplace. Our recent legislation to give statutory rights to Union Learning Representatives will ensure that this network can play an increasingly influential part. The network has shown that it is effective at reaching out to the lowest skilled and most disadvantaged groups in the workplace, and finding opportunities for them to develop their skills. Adults with low skills often wish to avoid drawing attention to their skill gaps, and do not wish to approach an employer or learning provider to seek help. The role of Union Learning Representatives has been expanded both through legislation (which came into force in April 2003), and by funding for the Union Learning Fund (which is to rise from £11 million in 2003/04 to £14 million in the next two years). These changes mean there will be more Union Learning Representatives, with more time to carry out their duties, and supported by improved products and services for promoting learning.

ACHIEVING THE BENEFITS OF AN INCLUSIVE WORKFORCE

2.37   We want to increase skill levels for all under-represented groups and encourage all individuals to improve their employability. Women's participation in the labour market is a crucial contribution to UK productivity. Women make up 44 per cent of the workforce but on average have fewer educational qualifications than men. The gender gap in qualifications is concentrated among those women who are over 40 and those who are employed part-time or not at all. This is a significant part of the skills deficit.[19]

---

19 Walby, S and Olsen W, (2002) *The impact of women's position in the labour market on pay and implications for UK productivity*, Report to the Women and Equality Unit

2.38 Women in work are concentrated in lower level non-manual occupations with 24 per cent working in administrative and secretarial occupations and 13 per cent in personal services occupations.[20] Women who work part-time may miss out on training opportunities offered by their employers. There have been significant increases in the overall level of skills in the British workplace, but their distribution is uneven. In particular the skill level of women in part-time work has not increased as much as that of full-time workers.

2.39 The difficulties of balancing family and work commitments can cause people to drop out of the labour market. New measures for working parents are aimed at helping them balance those responsibilities. This will help retain skills within the labour market, and help employers benefit from a broader labour force. The work-life balance campaign aims to increase take-up of employment practices that benefit business and help employees enjoy a better balance between work and other demands on their lives. This helps employers to recruit and retain skilled employees who might otherwise withdraw from employment.

20 Dench, S, Aston, J, Evans, C, Meager, N, Williams, M and Willison, R (2002) *Key indicators of women's positions in Britain*, Institute for Employment Studies

Chapter 3

Skills for Employers – the Sector Role

SUMMARY OF THIS CHAPTER

3.1　At the heart of the Skills Strategy is a powerful new drive, in each major sector of the economy, to identify and deliver the skills that employers need to raise productivity.

3.2　The new network of Sector Skills Councils – known as the Skills for Business Network – will lead that drive. Each Council will work with, and for, employers and employees in the sector they represent. The front runners are already showing what can be done. We want all of them to match that best.

3.3　We will:

　　a.　Expect each Sector Skills Council to deliver top quality analysis of international, national and regional trends in labour, skills and productivity in their sector. This will feed into the cycle for planning and funding the supply of training.

　　b.　Expect each Sector Skills Council to develop occupational standards defining the skills needed in their sector, as a basis for designing up-to-date, high quality courses and qualifications.

c. Expect each Sector Skills Council to seek to work with employers in order to broker a skills agreement for its sector, demonstrating employers' commitment to maintaining and improving the skills base. That agreement will set out a long term agenda for action on skills, tailored to the needs and priorities of each sector and derived from its unique business needs.

d. Ensure that Sector Skills Councils can engage effectively with the Learning and Skills Council, Regional Development Agencies and other funding agencies, through national and regional frameworks for skills action, to get real leverage over the allocation of public funds for adult skills.

e. Provide Government support, through the Sector Skills Development Agency, to provide development funding to back up and implement sector skills agreements.

THE ROLE OF SECTORS

3.4 The central theme of this strategy is the importance of identifying the skills that employers must have to support future business success, and doing whatever we can to ensure that the supply of training, skills and qualifications is responsive in meeting those needs.

3.5 Through the Regional Development Agencies (RDAs) and the regional partnership frameworks which they help to shape (notably the Frameworks for Regional Employment and Skills Action – FRESAs), we have a powerful mechanism for determining, region by region, the priorities for economic development and skills. Our proposals for strengthening regional skills planning are set out in chapter 7.

3.6 But that is not enough. Many companies operate nationally and internationally, not just locally and regionally. Table 3 illustrates this. For many purposes employers have a strong sense of local association. But they also identify with their sector and their supply chain, particularly in keeping up with leading-edge techniques, product or service innovation, knowledge transfer from new research, and all of the consequences that may have for future skills needs.

3.7 We want to ensure that employers have access to support through people who have a detailed understanding of their sector. RDAs have a close understanding of their region, but cannot be expected to have that same depth of understanding across each and every sector of the economy. Unless our approach to developing skills includes an understanding of where each sector is going, and what has to be done to match and exceed the best international productivity levels in that sector, we will not pitch our skills ambition at the right level. So we need both dimensions: regional and sectoral.

Table 3: Main focus of product markets at business level, by percentage of businesses in an industry, 2001

	Local	Regional	National	International	TOTAL
Food, drink and tobacco	13	19	54	13	100
Electrical, electronic and instrument engineering	6	14	45	35	100
Building, civil engineering	36	42	21	1	100
Retailing – specialised stores	58	19	19	4	100
Hotels	19	11	53	16	100
Restaurants and catering	72	17	8	2	100
Transport services	36	16	35	13	100
Financial services	28	19	36	18	100
Computer services	7	10	52	30	100
Architecture and engineering related business services	10	32	44	13	100
Total	39	21	29	10	100

Source: Geoff Mason (2003), *Enterprise product strategies and employer demand for skills: evidence from Employers Skill Surveys*, National Institute of Economic and Social Research (mimeo).

CREATION OF THE SKILLS FOR BUSINESS NETWORK

3.8 We will build the Skills for Business Network to fulfil the sectoral role. Sector Skills Councils (SSCs) are a means whereby employers can secure influence in shaping the supply of training and skills to meet current and future needs.

3.9 The full network will be set up by summer 2004. There will be around 25 SSCs covering the UK, replacing the 73 former National Training Organisations. Two Councils have been fully licensed to date, e-skills UK and the Science, Engineering and Manufacturing Technologies Alliance (SEMTA). Both have strong buy-in from the employers in their sectors. In addition, five 'trailblazers' are operating and a further 13 Councils are in development. The Sector Skills Development Agency (SSDA) is responsible for establishing the network, promoting the development of each Council and monitoring their performance. The SSDA acts as developer, co-ordinator and ambassador for the network. Table 4 shows the timetable for creating the network.

3.10 We and the SSDA will ensure that the way in which the Skills for Business Network is set up is rapid and straightforward. There have been concerns about delays and bureaucracy. There is a great deal to do to build the capacity of the network to sustain the prominent role that we envisage for it. But we will not compromise on the

Table 4: Timetable for setting up Sector Skills Councils

Phase 1 to April 2003	Phase 2 May – December 2003	Phase 3 January – June 2004
e-skills UK (Information and communication technologies and call/contact centres) **SEMTA** (Science, engineering and manufacturing technologies)	**Construction Skills** **Hospitality, Leisure, Travel and Tourism** **Automotive Services** (Sales, maintenance and repair of vehicles) **Energy and Utilities Skills** **SkillsactiveUK** (Sport and recreation) **Skills for Logistics** (Freight transport, storage and warehousing, courier services) **Skillset*** (Audio-visual industries)	**Cogent Plus*** (Oil and gas extraction, refining and chemical manufacture, polymers and nuclear) **Justice** (Prisons, immigration services – including detention centres, courts and secure escort services, police, probation, prosecution services, youth justice) **Skillfast-UK*** (Apparel, footwear and textiles) **Skills for Health** **Food and Drink** **Financial Services** **Proskills** (Process industries and manufacturing) **SummitSkills** (Building services and electro-technical, heating, ventilating, air conditioning, refrigeration and plumbing) **Lantra*** (Environmental and land-based industries) **Skillsmart*** (Retail) **Facilities Management** **GoSkills** (Passenger transport) **Lifelong Learning** (Post-16 education) **Social Care**

*Trailblazer SSC

standards that must be met before a licence is awarded to become an SSC. Every Council must represent a major step up in ambition, scope and effectiveness. One component of that is ensuring that each Council covers a sector which represents a sufficient proportion of the labour force to give it critical mass. The broad benchmark is 500,000 people. The SSDA is working with a wide range of bodies representing sub-sectors to support their incorporation within a sector of at least that size.

3.11　In setting up the network, the SSDA is seeking to incorporate a role for those groups which do not themselves meet the criteria to form a separate SSC, but nonetheless have an important part to play in defining skill needs for particular areas of employment. A prime example is those working in voluntary and community organisations. The Active Communities Unit in the Home Office is working with the Skills for Business Network and other partners to tackle the skills gaps of this sector to improve capacity. A specific voluntary and community sector skills strategy, building on this Skills Strategy, will be published by the Home Office in early 2004.

3.12　The Department for Education and Skills (DfES) has to date been the lead department for the SSDA, jointly sponsoring the Agency and the Skills for Business Network with the Devolved Administrations in Scotland, Wales and Northern Ireland, because the Agency and the Councils have a UK-wide remit. The Department of Trade and Industry (DTI) has also been closely involved in setting up the network, and will in future jointly sponsor the Agency, the network and sector-based activities.

3.13　The DTI has a strong sector focus through its business relations team. In some sectors, DTI has supported employer-led Innovation and Growth Teams, to identify and address the key productivity drivers for the sector. Some sectors support Industry Forums to improve the competitiveness and productivity of sector supply chains. The SSDA will increasingly become the body which brokers, co-ordinates and promotes the skills implications of sector-based activities on behalf of both departments, and engages with the key funding bodies in planning and delivering the SSC agreements. In doing so, it will also work with the range of Government departments which sponsor particular sectors such as transport, land-based industries or culture and media.

ROLE OF SKILLS FOR BUSINESS NETWORK

3.14　The Skills for Business Network must be built on excellent labour market information, as a basis for understanding skills and productivity gaps, and how they might be met. Drawing on national data collected by Government and its agencies, the network must become the authoritative source of sectoral and occupational data and projections. The SSDA has made a good start on this work. The results so far are given on its website at www.ssdamatrix.org.uk. A summary to illustrate the nature of the sectoral data available on skills and productivity is at annex 3. That table also summarises some of the key issues in tackling skills gaps in each sector, as a basis for continuing discussion and analysis with the network, employers, the Learning and Skills Council (LSC) and the RDAs.

3.15 Each SSC will have to start by ensuring that it has a rich, authoritative understanding of the skills and productivity trends in its sector, internationally, nationally and regionally. But the picture on skills is not static. So each Council should be collecting, publishing, and regularly updating on the web its analysis of skills gaps and trends. The SSDA will ensure a consistent approach across the network.

3.16 The core roles of the Skills for Business Network are:

a. Identifying and articulating the current and future skills needs of employers in their sector, at all levels from basic to advanced.

b. Developing, and keeping updated, national occupational standards which define the skills, knowledge and competences that employers require, and that training programmes and qualifications should deliver.

c. Engaging with colleges, training providers, universities and planning bodies to ensure they understand and act on sectors' skills needs.

d. Identifying the drivers of increased productivity in their sector, and the skills that will be needed to capitalise on these.

e. Reviewing the suitability of existing training programmes and qualifications to meet sector needs, and commissioning the development of new programmes where needed. This should underpin the proposals in chapter 4, to ensure the availability of high quality, up-to-date training programmes, suitable for the needs of adults in supporting a broad base of employability skills leading to a full level 2 qualification.

f. Contributing to joint work across the Skills for Business Network on generic and cross-sector skills. The SSDA is establishing cross-sector Boards to pursue that work. One priority is leadership and management, where the SSDA will have a key role in the new programme referred to at paragraph 2.17. A second is sustainable development, as a theme which needs to be addressed both in terms of the generic skills relevant to all sectors, and the skills specific to each sector, in understanding, developing and implementing sustainable technologies and working practices.

3.17 Chapter 5 explains in more detail the role of the Skills for Business Network and the SSDA in reforming qualifications and training programmes, working with the Qualifications and Curriculum Authority (QCA) and the LSC.

3.18   Over and above these core roles which we expect each SSC to undertake, the Skills for Business Network can potentially have a much larger impact through brokering voluntary collaborative action in their sectors. The network is not just a means of addressing the publicly-funded training supply side. It must become a means of brokering action by employers to meet each sector's needs.

3.19   In doing so, Councils must learn from the examples of excellent practice that already exist. Some of the most innovative work on skills in recent years has been developed through sector initiatives. The case studies below illustrate this. That is the standard all SSCs must match.

Case study 3: e-skills UK Sector Skills Council

e-skills UK was licensed by the Government in April 2003 as the SSC for IT, telecoms and contact centres.

e-skills UK brings together a powerful team of industry leaders, focused on solving the issues that no single company could address on its own. Board members include the Chief Executives or Managing Directors of IBM, Accenture, EDS, Hewlett Packard, Microsoft, Oracle and T-Mobile, and the Heads of IT at BT, Sainsbury's, Ford, John Lewis, the Inland Revenue and Morgan Stanley, as well as representation from smaller companies.

e-skills UK is concerned not only with the growth of the IT and telecoms industries, but with the e-skills of the UK at large – from the ability of businesses to understand the strategic implications of IT and become e-enabled, to the IT user skills individuals need to participate in the e-economy. For contact centre employers, e-skills UK is working to build on the UK's current strength as market leader in Europe to ensure the skills are available to compete successfully on a global scale for high value-added operations.

e-skills UK is working to link demand and supply of skills in key areas including:

- **Computer Clubs for Girls:** a programme which engages the music, publishing and software industries to introduce professional industry-standard technical skills into schools. The programme aims to change the attitudes and abilities of a generation of girls in terms of careers in IT.

- **e-skills Passports:** a single web gateway linking individuals requiring IT training and the myriad of training opportunities in the UK. Using the service, any individual in the UK can assess, log and improve their IT user skills against a framework of skills defined and recognised by employers. This facility also enables the mapping of all IT training and qualifications to the same, employer-defined structure of skills. Individuals can improve their value to employers, employers can target development programmes to those in need and Government can ensure publicly-funded training delivers the skills needed for employment.

- **Employers' Curriculum Forum:** bringing together employers and universities to create new degree courses that embrace leading-edge technical, business and interpersonal skills, and give the leaders of the future an understanding of the strategic value of technology to business.

Case study 4: Skillset Sector Skills Council

Skills Investment Fund

Skillset, the SSC (in development) for the Audio Visual Industries, was one of the first five trailblazer SSCs.

The UK's film industry is made up of a predominantly freelance and mobile workforce where high level craft, technical and creative skills are in high demand. The need to keep these skills up-to-date led to the establishment of the skills investment fund. This is made up of contributions from all film productions either based in the UK or in receipt of UK public funding. 0.5 per cent of the total production budget, up to a ceiling of £39,500, is collected by Skillset, which manages the fund on behalf of the film industry. The investment, currently totalling £1.9 million from 125 productions, is reinvested into training provision and assessment which meets industry agreed priorities.

The achievements of the skills investment fund include the strengthening of existing new entrant training schemes run by FT2 in England, Cyfle in Wales and Scottish Screen in Scotland. These schemes last from 18 months to 2 years and include wide ranging placements on productions, short course training, and assessment against the relevant Skillset Professional Qualifications (NVQ).

The skills investment fund has also been instrumental in the creation of the Assistant Production Accountant Scheme managed and run by the Production Guild of Great Britain and partnership-funded by the South East of England Development Agency. The scheme, which addresses a particular skills shortage in the industry, is run alongside subsidised places on short courses for up to 300 freelance production accountants and assistants.

SECTOR SKILLS AGREEMENTS[21]

3.20 We want each SSC, as it becomes fully operational, to consider the value of a sector skills agreement for its sector. Consistent with the overall approach of the Skills Strategy, it will be for employers not Government to determine, through their SSC, whether an agreement for collaborative action should be pursued. It is important to learn from past experience of both what has, and what has not, proved effective by

---

21 As noted in paragraph 3.12, the SSDA and the SSCs have a UK-wide remit. This section on sector skills agreements applies to England. The application of these proposals will need to take account of the different arrangements in the Devolved Administrations in Scotland, Wales and Northern Ireland.

way of collective action in different sectors of the economy. We also need to learn from experience in other countries. But working with the SSDA, the Government will strongly support and encourage such agreements where the SSC and the employers judge that such an agreement would be valuable. One of the roles of the Skills Alliance (see chapter 7) will be to oversee progress, not by taking a role in individual agreements, but by assessing the impact of the overall approach across sectors, and how it can be developed to achieve the greatest benefit.

3.21   One reason why individual employers do not invest in the skills of their workforce is because they fear that investing on an individual basis will not only cost more, but the staff (and therefore the value of their investment) may be poached by another firm which is not making a similar investment.[22] Overcoming that fear will require support for collaborative investment in skills amongst the employers in a given sector.

3.22   The nature of the action that is appropriate will vary from sector to sector. Different industries have already adopted a variety of approaches to promote collaborative action on skills, including licences to practise or operate, skills passports, sector training academies, voluntary training levies, collaborative training programmes, or action through the supply chain. A model of sector skills accounts may suit some sectors. In some cases, different agreements may apply to different parts of the sector. In all cases, it will be important to ensure that the agreement does not become a means of restricting entry to new companies, distorting competition or creating excessive burdens particularly for small and medium sized enterprises. Nor must it have the effect of discouraging or suppressing individual action by employers, but rather complement it.

3.23   We envisage that the agreements would cover:

a.   An analysis of sector trends, the drivers of productivity, any areas in which a 'low skills equilibrium' is apparent, and the consequent workforce development and skills needs to increase competitiveness over the medium to long term.

b.   A review of the current state of skills in the sector, identifying current skills gaps and latent skills shortages.

c.   A review of the range and quality of training provision available for the sector, and priorities for improvement. This would need to cover provision at all levels including generic employability skills, Modern Apprenticeships and Foundation Degrees.

d.   Identification of major cross-industry skills needs, particularly leadership and management and ICT.

---

22 See Department for Education and Skills (2003) *Developing a National Skills Strategy and Delivery Plan: underlying evidence*, paragraphs 50–55

e. An assessment of the scope for collaborative action by employers in the sector to tackle skills shortages; what form that action might best take; and the extent of agreement amongst employers and unions as to its desirability.

f. Close collaboration with the LSC and RDAs so that existing skills funding is prioritised to meet sector needs.

3.24 We will support such agreements in four ways:

a. The SSDA will provide some additional funding for the most credible and creative agreements brokered by SSCs, to contribute towards the costs of developing and implementing them. It will be able to fund the additional costs of, for example, brokering and trialling the agreement, designing passport schemes, setting up collective training programmes, negotiating the terms of a voluntary licence to practise, or designing bespoke training approaches.

b. In its continuing programme of sector-based training pilots, the LSC will give priority to working with those sectors or sub-sectors that demonstrate they are willing and able to develop agreements that will make a difference. Working with the LSC provides a route to access public funds for some of the direct costs of training programmes for regional and local delivery. The LSC has developed national sector training programmes with bodies representing employers in a range of sectors and sub-sectors, and at different levels. Those pilots have established some important principles for designing responsive training programmes, featuring work-based training, assessment of existing staff skills, packaging of training units to form qualifications which meet industry needs, and brokerage to source the training from suitable providers. The pilots are demonstrating high employer and employee engagement and high success rates.

c. Under the arrangements described in chapter 7, the results of sector skills agreements will feed through to regional and local planning and funding decisions on training supply. That is the crucial form of leverage enabling the models which emerge to be delivered in volume through the normal budgets of local LSCs. We do not want to set up a parallel funding system, alongside the LSC, to support mainstream training by sectors. That would only cause confusion and extra bureaucracy for learning providers. But we do want robust sector skills agreements to be a powerful influence on the existing allocation method, by building them into the FRESAs, which in turn set the framework for LSC decisions on what to fund. By this means, sector agreements will act as a turnkey to releasing funding more in line with business demand.

d. Where both employers and unions in an industry agree, we remain willing
    to use the existing powers under the Industrial Training Board (ITB) legislation
    to introduce training levies to pool the costs of training across employers
    (see paragraphs 3.28 and 3.29 below).

3.25 The main benefit of these agreements will be to engage partners representing
      both demand and supply in a compact that develops a shared analysis of the skills
      challenge for each sector, shared objectives for tackling it, collaboration in taking the
      necessary action, and the development of a demand-led method for allocating funds
      in response to employer needs.

3.26 With SSDA, we will start by working with a small number of SSCs who have the
      capacity to deliver the agreements, and where there is a commitment amongst sector
      employers to pursue the approach. We will evaluate carefully the experience of the
      first SSCs in delivering skills agreements, as a basis for extending the programme
      across the network.

3.27 At the same time, we will build a strong interface between the Skills for Business
      Network and the RDA and LSC operations, so that future sector skills agreements
      can gain direct leverage over the allocation of funds to training providers. It would
      be over-complex for every SSC to develop a regional delivery network of its own,
      to link with every RDA. Instead, the interface needs to work through:

      a. Each SSC working with the LSC nationally on the design of sector skills
          agreements, as discussed above.

      b. The SSDA establishing, on behalf of the Skills for Business Network, a regional
          network of representatives so that the collective voice of the SSCs can be
          integrated in regional and local discussions.

      c. Each RDA partnering with two or three SSCs, so that different RDAs are leading on
          liaison with different sectors, rather than every sector trying to link with every RDA.

      d. The LSC also identifying sector leads within the local LSC network.

THE FUTURE OF INDUSTRIAL TRAINING BOARDS

3.28 One form of collective sector action is a training levy. The 1964 Industrial Training Act
      enabled Industrial Training Boards (ITBs) to levy funds from employers to support
      training activity. The DfES is currently undertaking Quinquennial Reviews of the two
      remaining Boards – the Construction Industry Training Board (CITB) and the
      Engineering Construction Industry Training Board (ECITB). The reviews are assessing
      the continuing need for the Boards and the scope for improvements in their
      operation. Our conclusions from the first phase of the reviews are that the industrial
      training board approach and the levy suit the particular nature of the industries in

construction and engineering construction, and should remain. Reports on that first phase will be published shortly.

3.29 The Government has a manifesto commitment that, where both sides of industry in a sector agree, we will help them set up a statutory framework for training. Following that commitment, employer and trade union representatives from the print industry have been exploring whether a statutory approach would be an appropriate way forward. If the sector supports this, we are willing to use existing powers to create a new ITB for the print industry. However, the Quinquennial Reviews of the ITBs suggest that, while the statutory levy approach may suit some industries, it is unlikely to be a solution for many. We believe that the collaborative voluntary action that SSC can broker will be the appropriate route for most sectors.

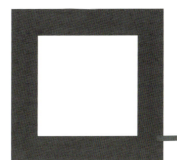

Chapter 4

Skills for Individuals

SUMMARY OF THIS CHAPTER

4.1 People are the key to a successful economy. We must put in place a framework that gives every young person a firm foundation and gives adults opportunities to develop their skills throughout their working lives. But learning and skills are not just about work or economic goals. They are also about the pleasure of learning for its own sake, the dignity of self-improvement, the achievement of personal potential and fulfilment, and the creation of a better society.

4.2 Our strategy aims to help people develop the skills they need for employment and personal fulfilment. But in making decisions about public funds we have to prioritise so that funding is targeted where it will make most difference. People learn for different reasons and in different circumstances. So, particularly at local level, we must support individual choice. Finally, people can face barriers and obstacles to learning that are not just financial. We need to support learners in different ways, offering information and advice, making courses accessible, helping with costs and fostering support from their employers.

4.3   To achieve these goals, the Government will:

a. Introduce a new entitlement to free learning for all those studying for their first full level 2[23] qualification as a skills foundation for employability.

b. Provide targeted support for higher level skills in priority areas to meet sectoral and regional needs.

c. Introduce a new adult learning grant of up to £30 a week for full time[24] learners studying for their first full level 2 qualification, and young adults studying for their first full level 3[25] qualification.

d. Improve information, advice and guidance services for adults so that people know what courses are on offer, and can get advice on which will best meet their needs.

e. Strengthen the range of opportunities for adults returning to education by:

i)   Ensuring that there is a coherent range of those learning programmes which promote personal fulfilment, community development and active citizenship, with funding clearly assigned to support them.

ii) Offering better opportunities in basic Information and Communications Technology (ICT) skills, by developing the range of free introductory courses available, and extending the tools for diagnosing and accrediting those skills.

SKILLS FOR INDIVIDUALS: WORK, LEISURE AND PERSONAL FULFILMENT

4.4   For individuals, skills are not just about work. They also serve essential social purposes. Achieving a fairer, more inclusive society depends on young people leaving school or college with the skills they need to work. Where they lack such skills, their exclusion is likely to be compounded during their lives.

4.5   So economic and social objectives are necessarily entwined. But skills serve wider purposes. For many people learning enriches their lives. They may enjoy learning for its own sake. Or it may make them better placed to give something back to their community, to help family and friends, to manage the family finances better, or help their children achieve more throughout their school careers.

TARGETING LEARNERS WITHOUT FIRST QUALIFICATIONS

4.6   Over 7 million adults in the workforce do not have a qualification at level 2. Those people are more likely to lack a skills foundation for employability and lifelong learning, and are less likely to get a secure, well paid job. In contrast, the higher wages paid to people with qualifications above level 2 offer more incentive to individuals and employers to invest in learning. The investment of public funds should be focused on

---

23 Full level 2 refers to a standard equivalent to 5 GCSEs at A* -C or a National Vocational Qualification at level 2.
     A combination of other vocational qualifications, of different sizes, may be required to reach this standard
24 Full time is a programme of at least 450 guided learning hours in a 12-month period
25 Full level 3 refers to a standard equivalent to two A levels or a National Vocational Qualification at level 3

helping people reach the level 2 platform for skills development, within a wider strategy which encourages up-skilling and re-skilling at all levels.

4.7 These considerations were reflected in the decision announced in the Government spending review in 2002 to set a new Public Service Agreement target at level 2. The target is to reduce by at least 40 per cent the number of adults in the workforce who lack level 2 qualifications by 2010; and working towards this, 1 million adults in the workforce to achieve a level 2 qualification between 2003 and 2006. To meet the target for 2010, three million more adults will need to benefit. Chart 2 shows recent trends in the number of economically active adults with a level 2 qualification, and the rate of change implied by the target.

Chart 2: Number of adults in the workforce with a qualification at or above level 2

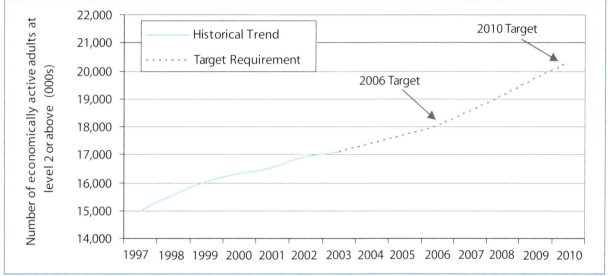

4.8 The 2010 target is ambitious, and represents an acceleration from the 2006 target. Achieving the necessary increase in demand from learners and employers is a major challenge. We believe that we are on track to achieve the 2006 target when account is taken of the flow of better qualified young people into the labour market. Through the reforms in this Skills Strategy, we intend to build the capability within the supply of training and skills to be able to achieve the faster rate of growth implied by the target between 2006 and 2010. By increasing the responsiveness of the supply of training and skills, while simultaneously acting to raise demand from employers and learners for skills, we expect that substantial increases in achievement by those with few or no qualifications will be secured.

Developing the Skills for Life Programme: Adult Basic Skills

4.9 We are already making good progress in tackling the problem of poor basic skills among adults through our *Skills for Life* programme. Well over a million learners engaged in literacy, language and numeracy courses between April 2001 and July 2002 and 319,000 adults achieved a national qualification. We are on track to meeting our target of 750,000 adults with better basic skills by 2004 and 1.5 million by 2007. Chart 3 shows progress made to date and the further increases needed.

4.10 But we cannot be complacent. There are still millions of adults in this country who lack the reading and maths skills that we expect of the average 11 year old. So over the next three years we plan to provide over 3 million learning opportunities delivered in ways that suit learners' circumstances. Ufi/**learndirect** uses e-learning to provide accessible, flexible and supported learning to those with *Skills for Life* needs.

4.11 Until now, basic skills have referred to literacy and numeracy. In today's society, we believe it is as important that everybody can also use Information and Communications Technology (ICT), particularly in the workplace. So we shall offer basic ICT skills as a third area of adult basic skills alongside literacy and numeracy within our *Skills for Life* programme.

4.12 We are developing the range of introductory ICT skills provision through UK online, Ufi/**learndirect** centres and other providers, to enhance the *Skills for Life* programme and more generally, to encourage adults who already have literacy and numeracy skills to develop basic ICT skills. We are developing an on-line ICT skills diagnostic tool, to help people assess their own level and need. We are also supporting the development by the e-skills UK Sector Skills Council (SSC) of an e-skills passport, which will support the accumulation of skills in a variety of settings. Our wider approach to e-learning and ICT use is set out in chapter 6.

Chart 3: Projected achievement on literary, numeracy and languages courses[26]

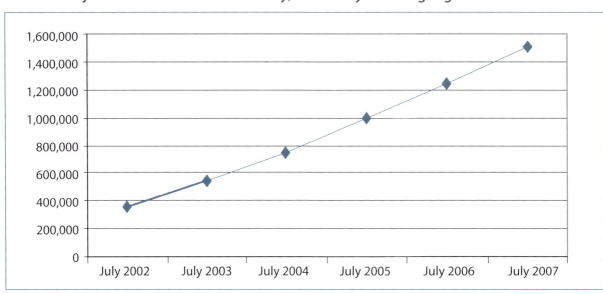

26 Based on current data from Learning and Skills Council, Offenders Learning and Skills Unit, Jobcentre Plus, and incorporates estimates of achievements through European Social Fund, Adult and Community Learning and Development Projects. This will be refined during 2003.

Entitlement to Foundation Skills for Employability

4.13 We must remove barriers faced by adults in gaining the foundation skills for employability represented by a full level 2 qualification. So we will create a new entitlement, enabling any adult in the labour force without a full level 2 qualification to have access to free learning for their first full level 2 qualification.

4.14 This new entitlement should send a very strong signal about the priority we attach to helping adults with few or no qualifications to achieve a good foundation of employability skills. We recognise that this will not by itself be enough to re-engage adults in learning. The *Skills for Life* programme has shown that the creation of entitlement to free learning does not guarantee take up. It will need to be supported by a wide range of other action, including information, learner support, qualification reform, and 'first step' opportunities. But it is one significant part in seeking to raise demand.

4.15 However, the numbers potentially involved are huge. So we need to manage the introduction and specification of the entitlement with care, so that it sensibly supports our policy priorities. We will do this in two ways. First, we will need clearly to define the entitlement, and how it fits within the wider policy framework. We intend that it will apply to those in the workforce or of working age who do not already have a full level 2 qualification, and who commit to trying to achieve one. Learners will be entitled to enrol on publicly-funded learning programmes leading to a full level 2 qualification offered by colleges and training providers. Within sector skills agreements, we will also apply the entitlement for those learning at work, while recognising that the terms of each agreement will be customised to the needs of each sector and that employers will be expected to contribute as well.

4.16 The second way in which we will manage introduction is through phasing over a period of time, in order that we can test out the impact on demand and the operational consequences. We expect to introduce the entitlement on a partial basis in 2004–05, and, subject to experience in that first year, proceed to roll out nationally from 2005–06 onwards. That will also give time to identify and develop those learning programmes and qualifications which will best support the policy objective of helping people gain foundation skills for employability.

SUPPORT FOR HIGHER LEVEL SKILLS: TECHNICIAN, HIGHER CRAFT OR ASSOCIATE PROFESSIONAL LEVEL

4.17 As noted in chapter 1, we have too few people with technician, higher craft and associate professional skills at level 3. These are some of the skills gaps that employers are most concerned about. So we will provide increased support for those who are developing their skills and qualifications to that higher level. We will develop this approach through the arrangements described in chapters 3 and 7 for identifying and tackling sectoral and regional skills needs.

4.18 As set out in chapter 3, SSCs will develop sector skills agreements which identify skills gaps at all levels, including higher level skills. In order to identify the sectoral priorities at level 3, we will ask the Sector Skills Development Agency (SSDA) and the Learning and Skills Council (LSC), in their joint work to support development of those agreements, to identify those sectors which have the greatest skills gaps at level 3. At the same time, local LSCs and Regional Development Agencies (RDAs) would identify regional priorities for developing skills at level 3. The conclusions of both the sectors and the regions would feed into the work of the regional skills partnerships described in chapter 7, through the Frameworks for Regional Employment and Skills Action (FRESAs). That will, in turn, guide the allocation of funds by local LSCs to colleges and training providers. Using the mechanism already developed by the LSC through its existing range of sector pilots, and subject to employer and sector commitments to contribute, priority access to some LSC funds would be provided to support the delivery of the agreed increase in level 3 qualifications.

4.19 This expansion of opportunities for higher level training, with strong employer backing, and reinforced by the new adult learning grants for young people studying full time to level 3 (see paragraphs 4.20 to 4.24), will create a powerful combination of new incentives to train.

FINANCIAL SUPPORT AND ADULT LEARNING GRANTS

4.20 We have already introduced reforms to encourage young people to continue in education and training beyond the minimum school leaving age of 16. Education Maintenance Allowances (EMAs) have helped many young people overcome financial barriers in pilot areas, offering up to £30 a week if they stay in school or college. EMAs will be extended nationally from September 2004.

4.21 Similarly, we recognise that young adults from low income backgrounds may need extra support entering higher education. The White Paper, *The Future of Higher Education*,[27] announced reforms to the student support framework, including targeted support to widen access, with help for those from disadvantaged backgrounds. Students from poorer backgrounds will be entitled to a new higher education grant of up to £1,000 a year. We aim to provide the full £1,000 to approximately 30 per cent of students. Students are entitled to loans which are repaid without any commercial interest rate.

4.22 We will increase financial support to help with the costs of learning for adults in further education through a new adult learning grant. We will offer a means tested grant of up to £30 per week to adults studying full-time for a first full level 2 qualification, and young adults studying full-time for a first full level 3 qualification. The new grants will be piloted from September 2003. We will trial the approach and evaluate the impact to establish, in

27 Department for Education and Skills (2003) *The Future of Higher Education*

the light of the conclusions of the next spending review, the best operational design with the intention of implementing a national roll out of adult learning grants.

4.23 Further education students, particularly those studying part-time, need access to support to help with the costs of learning. This will continue to be provided through the Learner Support Fund, towards the cost of books, materials, travel, childcare and examination fees. The level of help for each student will continue to be determined locally by colleges.

4.24 As announced in the March 2003 Budget, we are undertaking a cross-Government review of financial support for 16-19 year olds, including the financial incentives for young people to participate in education and training, and the interaction between this support and the case for any new minimum wage for 16 and 17 year olds. The review is to report in spring 2004.

CONSEQUENCES OF THE NEW SUPPORT AT LEVEL 2 AND LEVEL 3

4.25 This strategy is about ensuring that everyone has the skills they need. However, we have to strike the right balance and target a greater proportion of state funding towards priority groups, so those with the greatest need have opportunities to acquire relevant skills and qualifications. Over time, colleges and other providers will need to better focus their resources to support this aim. As set out in chapter 6, the consequence of prioritising some groups of learners is that other learners who have already achieved qualifications at level 3 or above and are seeking further qualifications at the same or lower levels will be expected to pay higher fees.

4.26 We believe this is the fairest way to manage participation overall in further education, and make productivity gains with public investment. On average, those with level 3 qualifications and above have higher incomes and are more likely to receive training at work for free. Moreover, adults in the UK contribute relatively little to the costs of their own learning when compared with other countries. In an OECD study, 19 per cent of British individuals undertook education and training that they had paid for, compared to 29 per cent in the US, and 37 per cent across the 11 OECD countries in the study.[28]

4.27 Where employers want training packages tailored to meet corporate needs, we would continue to expect them to meet some or all of the costs of skills training. This is already supposed to happen, but colleges often feel obliged to bear a higher proportion of the costs because of competitive or other pressures. We believe our proposals reflect both the proper balance of rights and responsibilities, and the major benefits which employers gain from a better skilled workforce.

4.28 If we are to focus resources on those without particular levels of qualification, we need to improve the information we have on people's existing qualifications. There is an

28 O'Connell (1999) *Adults in Training: An International Comparison of Continuing Education and Training* OECD: Paris

inherent difficulty in tracking the qualifications people already have. It will take time to develop new tracking systems. In the short term we propose a light touch screening of learners seeking different forms of support, drawing on existing data wherever possible. We do not want a major new bureaucracy. So we must ensure that we take a proportionate approach. Learners will be asked to declare the highest level of qualification they hold. In order to achieve this balanced approach, we will develop any necessary validation requirements alongside the phased introduction of the entitlement to free learning at level 2.

4.29 In the longer term, a Unique Learner Number could track learners' achievement as they progress, and create a single record of prior attainment. A feasibility study considering different approaches to introducing a Unique Learner Number will be completed at the end of July 2003. It is considering models of varying degrees of sophistication, including how it could build on the range of existing learner data like those available from the unique pupil number. So long as the practicalities of implementation and data confidentiality can be resolved, we will introduce at least the basic form of Unique Learner Number. This would provide a simple common identifier, reducing bureaucracy for learners by making it simpler for them to transfer between organisations, and simplifying assessment for any qualification-based entitlements.

4.30 The feasibility study is also considering more sophisticated models, which we hope to pursue over the longer term. At its most advanced, a Unique Learner Number could be an integral part of a learner database containing up-to-date information that can be accessed by a wide mix of learning providers and learners themselves.

INTEGRATING THE PRINCIPLES OF INDIVIDUAL LEARNING ACCOUNTS

4.31 We believe that the reforms in this strategy provide the essential elements which we previously sought to develop through the Individual Learning Account (ILA) scheme. The principles of the ILA scheme are still widely supported, despite the serious problems that led to the closure of the original programme. We are committed to sustaining those principles. We have examined carefully the lessons we must learn from the original programme, and have decided not to introduce another stand-alone ILA scheme, separate from the mainstream support for adult learning.

4.32 Instead, we have integrated those ILA elements that proved successful within the broader strategy, particularly through our proposals for a new entitlement to free learning at level 2 for those with few or no qualifications; improvements in learner support; broadening the range of training providers, so that we can bring within the scope of public funding those private providers who have something distinctive to offer and can meet the necessary quality standards; strengthening the range of first step and return to learn opportunities; improving information, advice and guidance for adults; and developing a Unique Learner Number.

BETTER INFORMATION, ADVICE AND GUIDANCE FOR LEARNING AND WORK

4.33 High quality and easily accessible information, advice and guidance (IAG) has an important role in helping people to understand the opportunities and support available. For young people, the expansion of the Connexions Service to cover all 47 LSC areas has begun to improve support and advice. Connexions provides a range of guidance and support, including careers advice to young people aged 13–19 years old, while targeting extra help to those who need it most to help remove barriers to learning.

4.34 Many adults get careers advice through their employers, and there are many private career consultancy firms providing guidance commercially. Universities and colleges have careers services for their students and Jobcentre Plus offers its clients advice about learning for work.

4.35 There are two nationally available IAG services – Ufi/**learndirect**, which gives information and advice both by telephone and internet on learning opportunities, and Worktrain, which is a website linking information on job opportunities with relevant training opportunities. There are IAG partnerships, funded through the LSC, in each local area, which bring together the existing IAG providers (careers service companies, Connexions, higher education, further education, voluntary and community organisations, libraries and Jobcentre Plus).

4.36 College and university students, and people at work, may well have a clear sense of how to access the service targeted specifically on their needs, and get excellent advice. But there is a gap for those adults who are not already in education or training, who cannot access advice at work, and who cannot afford to pay for advice. For them, the current array of existing services for adults, and the links between different parts, can be hard to understand. But they may be the people most in need of good advice.

4.37 We have taken some steps already to improve services for adults. The Ufi/**learndirect** national advice service handled nearly five million enquiries in 2002–03. The LSC has increased its funding for local IAG services. But a lot more needs to be done to improve the quality, consistency and visibility of provision. We will take the following action:

a. The LSC and Ufi/**learndirect** will integrate the **learndirect** national advice service with the work of the local IAG services. At present, national and local services do not always use each other's information or cross-refer clients to get the best advice. In future, all funding for the Ufi/**learndirect** national advice service and local services will be channelled through the LSC, supporting consistent planning and monitoring of services nationally and locally.

b. We will work with the LSC and Ufi/**learndirect** to define the range of IAG services which adults should be entitled to expect, and the standards to which those services should be delivered. This will be supported by a clear national brand, national marketing and local LSC marketing, so that users know what is available where they live.

c. We will continue to require all LSC-funded IAG providers to be accredited against the **'matrix'** standard through which we measure their quality and encourage improvements.

d. As announced in the 2003 Budget, the Department for Education and Skills (DfES) will work with the Department for Work and Pensions (DWP) to draw together the labour market information that employers and individuals require to make choices about learning and work. The DfES has begun work on improving information available on-line, and developing training for IAG practitioners in using labour market information.

4.38 We will publish, before the end of the year, an action plan for improvement which carries forward all of these elements.

OPPORTUNITY AND PROGRESSION IN LIFELONG LEARNING

4.39 For many people, qualifications are the best measure of achievement. They recognise their newly gained knowledge and skills, and they are widely understood. But this approach does not suit everybody. There are some with low skills who would welcome opportunities to improve their skills but would feel daunted by full qualifications. They want a 'first step' on the learning ladder or opportunities to try out learning before committing themselves. Reaching such reluctant learners is an important part of achieving our aims.

4.40 Others pursue learning for its own sake. They have enrolled in evening classes and extramural courses, with no intention of getting qualifications, but to broaden their horizons, expand their knowledge, and gain enjoyment from studying with others. There must continue to be a broad range of opportunities for those who get pleasure and personal fulfilment from learning. A civilised society should provide opportunities to enable everyone, including those who have retired, to learn for its own sake.

4.41 The range of lifelong learning opportunities still varies enormously across the country, and priorities for public funds vary. The LSC is now responsible for planning and funding the full range of this work, including programmes provided by colleges, Local Authorities and voluntary organisations. So for the first time, we have an opportunity to develop a consistent, coherent pattern of lifelong learning opportunities in each area across the country.

4.42 Working with the LSC, the National Institute for Adult and Continuing Education (NIACE) and other partners, we will take the following approach:

a. In each local area, the LSC will be responsible for securing the range of lifelong learning opportunities for adults suitable to meet local needs, as part of its overarching duty to secure learning and skills for young people and adults. The provision of such learning will be part of Strategic Area Reviews, to assess the current range, identify gaps and overlaps, and consider how it can be improved.

b. Adult and Community Learning programmes will be seen as an integral part of the wider learning opportunities for the area. But to safeguard the availability of these types of learning opportunities, the Government and the LSC will agree an overall indicative budget for the funds that should be used to support non-qualification-bearing programmes. Nationally, this will be based on the broad proportion of LSC funds currently spent on this type of learning. The budget will be able to cover, for example, family learning, learning for older people, active citizenship, community development, learning through cultural activities, and work with libraries, museums and art galleries.

c. From within that national indicative budget, the LSC will agree with each local LSC a minimum figure to spend on such learning activities. The distribution of these funds to each local LSC will need to be weighted to take account of socio-economic factors, and will need to recognise that the variation of current practice across the country means that it will take some time to achieve sensible consistency.

d. Each LSC will decide with its local partners – including Local Education Authorities, colleges, community and voluntary groups – the priorities for spending those funds in order to maximise the civic, social and cultural gain for the area. In many cases, there will also be money available from European Funds, neighbourhood renewal programmes, voluntary funds and other sources. The LSC is well placed to broker with its partners how those various funds can help achieve a coherent range of opportunities (including for example, the Workers' Educational Association and university extramural departments).

e. The LSC will specifically consider with its partners what first step and return to learn opportunities are available to encourage people back into learning. As a minimum, this will include opportunities through the 6,000 UK online and 2,000 Ufi/**learndirect** centres, colleges and neighbourhood learning centres.

f. The LSC will also consider whether there are private, voluntary and community providers, who are not currently supported through public funds, but who could make a distinctive and high quality contribution to the range of opportunities in the area. This could help widen participation, by extending the range of innovative and creative routes into learning. The LSC will seek to build the capacity of such providers to attract hard to reach adult learners.

g. We will build on the experience of the Adult and Community Learning Fund in developing an approach with the LSC, NIACE and others for ensuring that knowledge of what works in widening adult participation is disseminated and replicated.

IMPACT OF THE STRATEGY ON DIFFERENT GROUPS

4.43 Our Skills Strategy aims to ensure equality of access to opportunities by ensuring that public funds are focused on those most in need. Achieving basic skills reduces inequalities. Level 2 qualifications are associated with enhanced prospects and promotion of equality for some groups. Whilst 29 per cent of the workforce lacks a qualification at level 2 or above, this figure is much higher for the jobless (43 per cent), people with disabilities (up to 48 per cent), and older workers (34 per cent). People who work for employment agencies are also less likely to receive training (25 per cent, compared to 31 per cent overall). As noted in chapters 1 and 2, women are over-represented in a number of these disadvantaged groups.

4.44 Skills levels and participation in learning are also lower for some ethnic minority groups. Recent research shows a wide range of participation and qualification levels amongst ethnic minority groups. The average participation in learning by adults aged 16–64 was 78 per cent in 2001/02, compared to 84 per cent of those from African ethnic minority groups, but only 48 per cent of those from Bangladeshi ethnic minority groups.[29] These differences are also reflected in the qualifications that different groups hold. Compared with a national average of 16 per cent, 20 per cent of the minority ethnic adult population do not hold any qualifications; only 18 per cent of Chinese people lack qualifications, compared to 43 per cent of Bangladeshi people. The changes in this Skills Strategy will particularly help those with few or no qualifications, and those who currently have uneven access to learning.

4.45 There is already a strong commitment to ensure equality in the delivery of training and skills, through the requirements to promote equality placed upon the LSC, RDAs, and Jobcentre Plus. For example, the LSC is required to pursue equal access to opportunities for all under the Learning and Skills Act 2000, and through the LSC Remit and Grant Letters. The LSC is currently developing its new strategy for widening participation of adults in learning.

29 Aldridge, F and Tuckett, A (2003) *Light and Shade: A NIACE briefing on participation in adult learning by minority adults*. The report uses data from the Labour Force Survey 2001/02

4.46 The new entitlement to free learning at level 2, and the adult learning grants for those studying full-time, will help these disadvantaged groups of learners who are more likely to be low skilled. The new approach to Adult and Community Learning set out above will strengthen the opportunities available to a diverse range of people facing disadvantage. The combination of a strong LSC planning role, with more certain funding weighted according to socio-economic need, will enable the sector to continue to support and promote the needs of a wide range of people.

4.47 However, we know that currently learning opportunities are not always evenly taken up. While the numbers of men and women participating in work-based learning are broadly comparable, there are some sectors where the split is less even. So we welcome the Equal Opportunities Commission's recently announced investigation into occupational segregation in training and work, focusing particularly on Modern Apprenticeships. We invite them to treat their remit broadly, considering the range of vocational learning opportunities available, so that the benefits of the reforms set out in this White Paper are fairly distributed.

4.48 We want to safeguard a wide range of learning opportunities for pensioners. There is good research evidence[30] that older learners can benefit substantially from continuing to learn. For many, it represents an important form of social activity. There are benefits to mental and physical health. It may help them support learning within the family or community, as well as pursuing hobbies and leisure interests. While strengthening support for skills, training and qualifications which will support our wider economic goals, we want at the same time to ensure the continued availability of learning opportunities for pensioners which give so much benefit and pleasure. At present, there is wide variation between different areas in the range of learning available, and the fees that are charged for it. It is right that local discretion should remain. But we expect pensioners to benefit substantially from the arrangements for safeguarding funding for leisure learning, and that in all areas learning for pensioners would be one of the priorities to be pursued through the new planning and funding agreements.

4.49 We recognise the importance of ensuring that students with learning difficulties or disabilities have an equal opportunity to participate and achieve in learning. The LSC is currently undertaking a review of additional learning support funding. This will develop a common funding approach offering a clearer, fairer mechanism for supporting learners with learning difficulties or disabilities. The review will consider support across further education, Work Based Learning for Young People, Adult and Community Learning and school sixth forms.

30 Dench, S and Regan, J (2000) *Learning in Later Life: Motivation and Impact*, DfEE Research Report 183

SKILLS FOR MIGRANTS

4.50 As the working age population reduces across Europe, competition for internationally mobile, highly skilled people will intensify. It is essential that the Government ensures that immigration policy supports efforts to attract and retain internationally mobile, highly skilled people and key workers. People who settle in this country from overseas can play an important role in meeting skills shortages. In order to maximise that potential, we must ensure that the obstacles to their integration into the workforce are tackled. Through the Nationality, Immigration and Asylum Act 2002, we will ensure that, through the proposed citizenship and language programmes, those with a route to British Citizenship will have learned the information and skills they need to integrate fully in society.

4.51 Other actions in hand to enhance the role played by migrants in contributing to economic productivity are:

a. The Highly Skilled Migrant Workers programme was recently strengthened to attract more skilled individuals to the UK.

b. We are considering ways to retain overseas maths and science graduates in the UK.

c. The Working Holidaymakers Scheme is being reviewed.

d. The Home Office is setting up a new website to provide better information on the various legal migration routes into the UK.

e. We will consider introducing schemes to offer temporary work permits for those with lower level skills in sectors where needed. Such programmes are already operating in food processing and hospitality.

4.52 The National Academic Recognition Information Centre is working with the five local LSCs in London, to offer a more streamlined process for recognising overseas qualifications for those with vocational skills and qualifications at skilled manual and supervisory levels, and supporting them to get additional training to fill any skills gaps in order to achieve equivalent UK qualifications.

Chapter 5

Reforming Qualifications and Training Programmes

SUMMARY OF THIS CHAPTER

5.1   Our goal is that learning programmes and the qualifications that accredit them will respond fully and quickly to the skill needs of employers. All will be of high standard and provide clear routes to employability and progression for the learner. This revitalised system will equip many more people with the various levels of craft, technical and associate professional skills essential for economic success.

5.2   The redesign of learning programmes and qualifications is therefore at the heart of the Skills Strategy. The Qualifications and Curriculum Authority is working with the Sector Skills Development Agency, the Learning and Skills Council and other UK partners to take this work forward.

5.3   We will:

   a.   Ensure that learning programmes enable all young people to develop the skills, attitudes and attributes that employers seek.

   b.   Create programmes of vocational education and training from age 14 up to higher education, which support progression through the vocational route.

   c.   Encourage more 14–19 year olds to study maths and science.

d. Raise the quality and effectiveness of Modern Apprenticeships as the primary vocational option for young people, and lift the age cap so that more adults can benefit from these 'earn and learn' opportunities.

e. Create an employer-led qualifications system for adults that responds quickly to changing skill needs and recognises achievement of units as well as opportunities to gain whole qualifications.

f. Develop a credit framework for adults.

g. Give adults with few or no qualifications access to broad programmes that develop the foundation of employability skills.

Goals for the Qualifications Framework

5.4 Employers and learners will not get the skills they need unless training programmes and qualifications are fit for purpose. To achieve that, we need all the steps in the following sequence to work effectively:

- Identify clearly the skills which employers need to support future productivity, and which learners need to support sustainable employability.

- Translate those skill needs into standards for designing learning programmes which are kept fully up-to-date.

- Deliver the learning programmes in the way that best develops the skills, with the flexibility to meet different learners' needs.

- Base learning programmes on defined units, allowing adult learners and employers to combine units to meet their own needs, and to build over time towards qualifications.

- Ensure qualifications are robust and reliable measures of what the learner knows, understands, and can do.

- Ensure widespread understanding of the level of achievement which each qualification represents.

- Streamline the assessment process.

- Make assessment tools widely available to allow learners to assess their existing knowledge, understanding and skills, so that they can focus on training to fill gaps rather than repeating what they already know.

5.5 To achieve this requires clarity in the roles of three major contributors:

a. The Skills for Business Network will ensure that skill needs are accurately identified and translated into occupational standards as the basis for vocational qualifications in their sector. These standards set out the skills and competences which training programmes and qualifications should cover in order to guarantee that learners have the skills needed for successful employment.

b. The Qualifications and Curriculum Authority has responsibility for maintaining the rigour and fitness for purpose of the national qualifications framework. It accredits qualifications based on the learning and development necessary to achieve the occupational standards confirmed by appropriate assessment methods.

c. The Learning and Skills Council plans and funds the training providers so that learners and employers can undertake the learning programmes and assessments they want, and thereby gain qualifications in ways that are efficient, effective and responsive to needs.

5.6 This chapter is structured in three main blocks:

- Reform of vocational routes for young people aged 14–19, and preparation for employability, including mathematics, science and enterprise.

- Reform of the Modern Apprenticeships programme, as the leading work-based route to employability skills for young people.

- Reform of qualifications and training programmes for adults.

VOCATIONAL ROUTES AND EMPLOYABILITY SKILLS FOR YOUNG PEOPLE

The Tomlinson Review

5.7 As part of its remit to advise on the development of programmes and qualifications, the Working Group on 14–19 Reform, chaired by Mike Tomlinson, will advise by July 2004 on the development of more coherent vocational programmes. The Group is considering how to tackle the fragmentation of vocational courses and qualifications, improving the transparency and effectiveness of progression routes, and developing a broad base of skills and knowledge needed to underpin vocational specialisation and progression.

5.8 The Group's work will include:

a. Proposals for engaging employers in the development and delivery of a 14–19 framework which supports effective learning, while ensuring that the skill requirements of the workplace are met.

b. Development of a common template for 14–19 learning programmes. This will combine the specific knowledge, skills and understanding needed for particular sectors and careers with:

i)   the generic skills, attributes and knowledge essential to underpin progression, further learning, employment and adult life; and

ii) supplementary learning which enriches and broadens the specialist programme (for instance, through mathematics programmes tailored to meet the needs of engineers).

c.   Clear progression routes. All young people should be able to embark on programmes which can lead to at least level 3 in their chosen specialisation. The expansion of Foundation Degrees will extend the scope for progression into higher education from vocational programmes. The Group will consider how to ensure that 14–19 programmes offer a good preparation for these and other forms of higher learning.

d.   Effective delivery early in the 14–19 phase of key skills and other personal and interpersonal skills.

e.   Making better use of further education-based full-time programmes to create a distinctive approach to occupational learning to complement work-based training.

f.   Developing broadly-based vocational programmes with sufficient occupational relevance to lead directly to employment, while also offering a preparation for progression into higher education.

5.9   The Working Group intends to publish shortly a progress report outlining its early thinking, and an interim report in January 2004. It will publish its final report six months later.

Mathematics and Science in School, College and University

5.10 Providing young people with a good foundation in maths and science is essential if we are to meet the demand for higher level technical, scientific and professional skills.

5.11 The Government is committed to ensuring that all young people leave compulsory education with an understanding of the importance of science and technology. We will build on the reforms we have already made to the teaching and learning of these subjects in primary schools and in Key Stage 3. Maths and science will remain compulsory at Key Stage 4 in the school curriculum. The Qualifications and Curriculum Authority (QCA) has just completed a review of the current programme of study for science, to set a core content suitable for all learners, and is consulting on the outcomes. The aim is a coherent programme of study that underpins all science GCSEs.

5.12 The national network of science learning centres, being developed with the Wellcome Trust, will give science teachers the opportunity to strengthen their subject expertise and develop innovative teaching methods. Our new Further Education Standards Unit has identified science and mathematics as priorities in developing good practice frameworks for teaching and learning.

5.13 We have made good progress in implementing the recommendations from Sir Gareth Roberts' review of science, engineering and technology.[31] To encourage more students to take science degrees such as physical sciences, engineering and technology, we are making a sustained investment in science laboratories, research and teaching and learning. We are piloting different approaches to bridging the gap between students' prior knowledge and the requirements of degree courses. The Department for Education and Skills (DfES) is carrying out a mapping review of science, engineering, maths and technology initiatives to see how they can be better co-ordinated. The Department of Trade and Industry (DTI) is taking forward a strategy to improve women's representation in science, engineering and technology, including a resource centre to help women returners get jobs in these areas.

5.14 We will set up a National Centre of Excellence in Mathematics. Professor Adrian Smith, who is leading a review of post-14 maths education, will be putting forward proposals for the centre in autumn 2003.

5.15 However, the problems with maths in this country are longstanding and there is no simple way of boosting interest and achievement in the subject. The report of Professor Smith's review will be critical in developing a strategy. In his work so far, Professor Smith has confirmed a skills shortage in maths and related quantitative disciplines. The shortage relates to the ability to use, communicate and understand maths commonly needed in the workplace and essential for many practitioners in science, technology and engineering. Among the options he is considering are:

a. Providing students with maths courses appropriate to their needs, interests, current progress and level of understanding. Too many are on inappropriate courses leading to drop-out, boredom or both. GCSE maths is not sufficiently motivating for some students. Teachers are not always able to make useful connections with other subject areas.

b. Encouraging schools, colleges, universities and training providers to collaborate to raise the quality of maths teaching, and boost continuing professional development for teachers.

c. Giving greater attention to maths in careers education. Many students are unaware of the economic benefits of possessing good maths qualifications, and their value in undertaking growing numbers of degree courses.

Enterprise and employability skills for young people

5.16 Employers have consistently said that too many young people are not properly prepared for the world of work. This was a concern frequently raised in the Skills Strategy consultations. In particular, they may lack skills such as communication

---

31 Sir Gareth Roberts (2002) *SET for Success*, Final report of Sir Gareth Roberts' Review

and teamwork, and attributes such as self-confidence and willingness to learn that are of growing importance across a range of jobs. The best grounding in these skills depends on a strong partnership between schools and employers so that pupils see the relevance and application of the skills they are learning and gain an understanding of the needs of employers and the demands of the workplace.

5.17　DfES' Strategy and Innovation Unit has been undertaking a review of these generic skills, which are a major part of employability, to look at how they are best identified and developed. There is much already in the Government's programme of education reform that will foster these skills and attributes. Development of social and emotional competence at Foundation Stage, the new broader approach to primary education, the strategy for improving teaching and learning in secondary education and the learning and skills sector, and the wider key skills programme all have an important part to play. In developing and implementing principles of teaching and learning for all phases, and in the design of extra-curricular and out of school activities, we will make sure that teachers are equipped to make the most of opportunities to improve these skills. The strategy document *14–19: Opportunity and Excellence* confirmed our intention that all pupils at Key Stage 4 should undertake work-related learning, including the development of enterprise capability.

5.18　The review by Sir Howard Davies found that pupils' involvement in enterprise activities was likely to develop the skills and confidence they would need in employment.[32] Following the review, we have made available £60 million from 2005–06 to deliver enterprise education in secondary schools. By 2006 all Year 10 pupils will have the opportunity to experience five days' enterprise learning, helping to develop the knowledge, skills and attitudes for enterprise capability, financial capability, and economic and business understanding. Enterprise advisers will work with 1,000 secondary schools in deprived areas to give extra support to the enterprise education agenda.

5.19　The entitlement to enterprise learning will build upon the work already in hand to strengthen links between schools and employers and improve the quality of work-related learning. Over 95 per cent of pupils at Key Stage 4 already benefit from up to two weeks of work experience. The aim is that all should have the opportunity to do so. In 2003/04, we will test new ways of engaging employers in the learning of 14–19 year olds so that we can deliver a comprehensive range of vocational and practical opportunities in ways that suit the needs of local employers. We have designated over 1,400 specialist schools in subject areas including business and enterprise, technology, science, and mathematics and computing. Each specialist school has to show how

32　Davies, H (2002) *A Review of Enterprise and the Economy in Education*

business will contribute to development of the specialist curriculum or play an active part in the school's governance and management arrangements.

5.20 So by these various means, a lot is already being done to develop employability skills throughout the school curriculum and beyond. That needs to continue, in view of the central importance of those skills in meeting employers' needs. We believe that the partnership of the QCA, Learning and Skill Council (LSC) and Sector Skills Development Agency (SSDA) outlined earlier in this chapter can play a pivotal role in pursuing that work, in the light of the DfES Strategy and Innovation Unit's work. All of them have a close interest in employability skills, and they are well placed to draw together the threads of existing activity into a more systematic approach. So in carrying forward their agenda, collectively and individually, we look to the three organisations to define employability skills consistently, and seek to integrate the development of these skills into teaching and learning programmes and wider activities to develop individual skills and competence. In doing so, they will need to work with the Working Group on 14–19 Reform, because effective skills development is central to their remit. They will also need to consult with leading employers, and work with the Modern Apprenticeship Task Force, to ensure that further action is fully informed by what employers see as the gaps and areas for improvement, and that employers are involved as champions for improvement.

MODERN APPRENTICESHIPS

5.21 Modern Apprenticeships are central to our drive to improve workplace skills, particularly at craft, supervisory and technician level. Historically, the absence of apprenticeships for young people has been a major contributor to our skills gaps. We want apprenticeships to be the primary work-based vocational route for young people, giving them an excellent skills foundation, and designed with employers. Our target is that by 2004, 28 per cent of young people will start a Modern Apprenticeship by age 22.

5.22 Young people not yet ready to enter a Modern Apprenticeship will be able to join the new Entry to Employment (E2E) programme focused on individual development needs. Working with the Connexions Service, E2E will offer help with literacy, numeracy and information and communications technology (ICT) skills and the full range of support needed by low-achieving or disengaged 16-18 year olds, to help them enter a Modern Apprenticeship, employment or further education. We will examine, with those delivering Modern Apprenticeships, the extent to which some young people at age 14 may wish to focus their choice more substantially on the vocational option, so that they have a stronger foundation to progress directly into an apprenticeship post-16.

5.23 Our best Modern Apprenticeship programmes already match the best in the world. But there have been concerns about the quality of some programmes, the completion rates, and the wide variation between sectors in the quality of training and outcomes. We must ensure that all Modern Apprenticeships are of sufficiently high quality to attract many more learners and employers.

5.24 The LSC is addressing this. The main elements of its quality improvement programme are:

a. Boosting capability by encouraging the most successful employers to expand their training provision beyond their own immediate needs.

b. Fostering collaboration between training providers, particularly Centres of Vocational Excellence, and establishing high quality providers to replace those that have no reasonable prospect of meeting minimum standards.

c. Providing better training for staff delivering Modern Apprenticeships, particularly those involved in arranging and delivering learning leading to the new technical certificates.

d. Developing, with the Sector Skills Councils, guidance for those sectors with no tradition of apprenticeships on how to deliver good workplace learning.

e. Supporting sectors that want to develop stronger progression routes from Modern Apprenticeships to higher level vocational qualifications, including Foundation Degrees, ensuring that different funding systems do not create unnecessary barriers.

5.25 At the same time as improving standards, we need to raise the profile of Modern Apprenticeships, engage more employers in providing them, and ensure that they meet employers' needs. The LSC is working with the Modern Apprenticeship Task Force, chaired by Sir Roy Gardner, to address this by:

a. Encouraging employers to provide more Modern Apprenticeship placements, with a national employer recruitment campaign.

b. Recruiting more public sector apprentices with targets for each Government department.

c. Ensuring that qualified young people get better information about vacancies, for example through a dedicated website.

d. Encouraging employers to work together to expand the number of learning places, for example through Group Training Associations. Associations of employers can broker access to work-based learning facilities, help small businesses to share training resources, and increase substantially the impact of their investment in skills.

5.26 The Skills Strategy consultation highlighted two specific concerns about the design of Modern Apprenticeships – the place of key skills,[33] and the age cap which limits participation to those aged 24 and under. We have considered both of these concerns.

5.27 Our aim is to equip all Modern Apprentices with literacy and numeracy skills. We want apprentices and their employers to have access to best practice in key skills teaching and learning, and to reliable and flexible assessment methods. We will:

   a. Develop successor arrangements to the Key Skills Support programme, to share best practice.

   b. Provide training and advice on innovative approaches to basic and key skills.

   c. Make on-demand and ICT-based assessment more widely available, with on-line test delivery and assessment on offer to all training providers.

   d. Invite sectors to add key skills units in their National Vocational Qualifications and external tests in their technical certificates.

   e. Secure a level playing field, both between Modern Apprenticeship frameworks and between work-based learning and the full-time further education route, for the funding of basic and key skills learning.

5.28 On the age cap, public funding for Modern Apprenticeships is currently limited to those aged 24 and under. Many sectors are concerned that this age cap is a significant barrier to meeting skill needs. We recognise the force of these arguments, and agree that the apprenticeships approach has much to offer for adults.

5.29 So we are committed to removing the age cap. As a first step, we will change the rules with immediate effect so that young people who start their Modern Apprenticeship at any point up to their 25th birthday can complete it. Beyond that, the implementation of this change will need to be managed over a period of time. Firstly, the current budget for Modern Apprenticeships is limited, so we need to discuss with the LSC the scope for redeploying and making better use of funds over time to support expansion through development of the budgets for work-based learning.

5.30 Secondly, we need to consider how far the design of Modern Apprenticeships needs changing to reflect the different needs of adults. The Modern Apprenticeship model was designed to meet the needs of younger learners, and we do not want to compromise its rigour. So the same standards need to apply, and the same targeting on those who need help to raise their skills and qualifications. But adults have a higher base of existing skills, knowledge and competence. The design of Modern Apprenticeships for adults should reflect this through greater flexibility in the way the principles are applied.

---

33 For the purposes of Modern Apprenticeships, the key skills are: communication; application of number; information technology (IT); working with others; improving own learning and performance; and problem solving.

5.31 To take this forward, we will invite the Sector Skills Councils (SSCs) to review, with employers and others including the QCA, how they would like to design and implement a Modern Apprenticeship programme for adults in their sector, and come forward with proposals. That work would form part of the sector skills agreements discussed in chapter 3. As well as looking at design issues, it would cover the contributions which the employers themselves would make to the costs, and ways of securing high standards combined with high levels of retention and achievement.

FOUNDATION DEGREES AND SKILLS DEVELOPMENT IN HIGHER EDUCATION

5.32 *The Future of Higher Education* White Paper published in January 2003 stated the Government's intention to focus the expansion of higher education through Foundation Degrees. Foundation Degrees are employer-focused degrees that offer specific job-related skills. There are around 12,000 Foundation Degree students. A prospectus, due to be published in the autumn, will set out how we will achieve a major expansion over the next five years with the help of a new task force chaired by Professor Leslie Wagner, Vice-Chancellor of Leeds Metropolitan University.

5.33 *The Future of Higher Education* announced that universities would receive more support to share the results of their research with industry. This will help strengthen university-industry engagement. The Skills for Business Network and the relevant higher education subject networks will be encouraged to work together to ensure that curricula and course material keep pace with changing business practice and to offer opportunities for students to gain work experience. The Higher Education Funding Council for England (HEFCE) will develop a strategy for workplace learning to overcome barriers to this mode of delivery and secure wider employer buy-in to higher education.

5.34 A £1 million programme is being run through the Employability Skills Enhancement Team, funded by HEFCE, to disseminate best practice in employability skills. It works with the Learning and Teaching Support Network to involve subject professionals across higher education.

QUALIFICATIONS AND LEARNING PROGRAMMES FOR ADULTS

5.35 The consultation on the Skills Strategy highlighted widespread concerns that vocational qualifications for adults are too inflexible. But it also showed a large measure of agreement about what needs to change. We will maintain our focus on broad and coherent programmes of study for young people. However, for adults we will offer greater flexibility to combine different units, while keeping a clear qualifications structure that assures the currency of qualifications in the labour market.

5.36 Since December 2002, the QCA has been leading a joint review, with the SSDA and the LSC, of vocational qualifications with partners across the UK. It is the first time those bodies have worked together so closely, and we intend that joint working to set the pattern for the future.

5.37 Drawing on their work to date, and the approach already developed in some sectors, we intend to undertake far-reaching reform of the system, based on the following elements:

a. **National occupational standards and industry-led curricula**. National occupational standards are the template around which vocational qualifications should be designed. But in some sectors, it has taken up to two years to develop the standards, by which time industry practice may already have changed. National occupational standards must be developed quickly and kept up-to-date. They should be internationally benchmarked to bring best practice to the UK, written in plain English and freely available.

b. **Unitisation**. Wherever appropriate, qualifications will be divided into identifiable units. There will be further encouragement for qualifications that combine mandatory and optional units to meet industry needs. By offering simpler, clearer stepping stones, units will encourage learners to progress towards whole qualifications. Learners and employers will be able to use combinations of units as the basis for training programmes which suit their needs, with training providers tailoring courses to meet the skills requirements of the learner and employer.

c. **Streamlined accreditation**. Under current arrangements each new qualification is accredited by QCA. The QCA has streamlined the process to speed up accreditation. It will review more fundamentally its approach to regulation, taking into account lessons learned from monitoring awarding bodies and their qualifications. Consultation to date suggests that a substantial shift towards quality assurance based on risk assessment would be welcome.

d. **Vendor qualifications**. In sectors such as IT, the certificates offered by companies to recognise proficiency in using their products are highly valued. The best of those certificates should be recognised in the national qualifications framework. A unit-based approach will offer greater opportunities to incorporate high quality vendor and employer qualifications or units into the national framework.

e. **Rationalisation of qualifications**. The QCA and the Skills for Business Network will keep under review the qualifications available in each sector and remove qualifications that no longer meet the needs of a changing market while making sure that gaps are filled.

f. **Recognition of existing skills and knowledge**. Training programmes, particularly those provided for employers, should start by assessing people's existing knowledge and skills, so that skills gaps can be identified and training targeted at filling those gaps. This 'assess/train/assess' model is well established in college provision for work place delivery of National Vocational Qualifications, and is the norm in the LSC sector pilots and the Employer Training Pilots. The LSC will develop a network of assessors to conduct initial assessments, identify gaps and broker appropriate training in the workplace.

g. **Simplified assessment systems.** The QCA will simplify the regulatory criteria for vocational qualifications to ensure the best match between assessment and content. This will remove unhelpful barriers between National Vocational Qualifications and other vocational qualifications.

h. **Better communication.** The agencies will work together to communicate the benefits of vocational learning and the flexibility of the qualifications framework to all stakeholders.

5.38 This major programme of work will be guided by a Joint Steering Group, chaired by QCA's Chief Executive. The QCA, with the SSDA and the LSC, will publish a joint paper giving details of the proposed approach later in summer 2003.

5.39 The consultation on the Skills Strategy has shown widespread support for developing a national credit framework for adults. This is seen as a way of offering the greatest flexibility and responsiveness, with units of qualifications being assigned credit using a standard system. Supporters argue that adult learners can more easily build up units of credit over time towards qualifications, transferring that achievement between different providers if they wish, and having more choice in the units of qualifications they combine. Employers can put together units of qualifications drawn from different sources to form the training programme that best suits their needs.

5.40 Building on the preparatory work already undertaken, we believe that the time has come to commit to developing a credit framework for adults. In doing so, we recognise that there are many issues of policy and practice still to work through. The policy framework must, in particular, ensure that the programme of learning leading to a qualification has some rationale and progression opportunities for the learner, and is not just a random collection of units. And we must be clear how such a credit framework aligns with the development of a credit system in higher education. Assigning a credit value to the full range of existing units in the national qualifications framework represents a formidable task. So we propose to start by inviting the bodies which award the largest number of qualifications to adults to collaborate, under the aegis of the QCA and key partners, in a joint programme to develop a shared approach to a credit system which could be expanded over time towards a national credit framework. Those discussions would need to include the policy parameters and the scope for mutual recognition of units.

5.41 This approach would apply particularly to adult learning. Credit frameworks for young people raise quite different issues, which will be considered separately in the light of Mike Tomlinson's review of future 14–19 strategy. We will ensure however that any system for adults takes account of developing policy for 14–19 year olds, including progression through from initial to adult learning.

ROLE OF SKILLS FOR BUSINESS NETWORK

5.42 The SSDA and the Skills for Business Network are inheriting responsibility for defining national occupational standards from the National Training Organisations. We expect to make early decisions about future arrangements for the funding of that work.

5.43 We will invite the Skills for Business Network to work with the QCA to review the qualifications available in each sector as a basis for:

a. identifying which are most suitable to help adults develop the level 2 foundation skills for employability needed in their sector; and

b. where there are gaps, to work with awarding bodies to develop new qualifications.

5.44 The LSC sector pilots have demonstrated how training programmes focused on the needs of both learners and employers can successfully be developed and implemented. That is the approach we want the SSCs to build on.

ADULT BASIC SKILLS

5.45 The Government's *Skills for Life* programme already offers free support for all adults who wish to improve their literacy, language and numeracy skills. This is a central part of helping those who lack the essential skills for employment. All literacy, English for speakers of other languages, and numeracy provision is based on national standards, backed up by a core curricula and national qualifications.

5.46 We want to integrate these skills into the new workplace-based vocational programmes. During 2003 we will support those who develop or deliver programmes in the workplace with an interactive web-based programme that links the national standards and core curriculum to 142 different occupational standards. This will ensure that literacy, language and numeracy skills at the appropriate level can be embedded and developed more effectively through vocational programmes. Over time, we want to converge support for adult basic skills in literacy, numeracy and ICT into the wider programme of support to help adults get the foundation skills for employability, so that those foundation skills will contain a core of key skills alongside other sector-specific and general skills.

Chapter 6

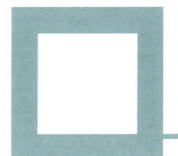

Reforming the Supply Side – Colleges and Training Providers

SUMMARY OF THIS CHAPTER

6.1   Previous chapters have set out how we will seek to respond to, and raise, the demand for skills, training and qualifications from employers and individual learners. But to achieve our goals, we must also improve the supply of skills, so that colleges and training providers are more responsive to that demand. In the previous chapter we saw how reform of the qualifications framework will help. This chapter considers the role of providers.

6.2   There are four principles underlying our approach to improved publicly-funded training provision for adults. It should:

- Be led by the needs of employers and learners.

- Be shaped by the skill needs prioritised in each sector, region and locality.

- Make the best use of Information and Communications Technology (ICT) to deliver and assess learning.

- Give colleges and training providers maximum discretion to decide how best to respond to needs.

6.3 We propose four key changes to achieve this:

- Wider choice for employers and learners of publicly-funded providers of adult skills and training.

- Increased range of ICT and e-learning resources.

- Reform the funding system to give incentives for providers to be more responsive, while cutting bureaucracy.

- Help to colleges and training providers to build their capacity to offer a wider range of support for local employers.

BACKGROUND

6.4 Many colleges and training providers already deliver flexible skills training very successfully. Over half of all general further education colleges have developed Business Development Units to offer bespoke training to employers.[34] One example is Learn@Work delivered by West Nottinghamshire College (see case study 5). But while colleges generally feel they have good links with employers, 90 per cent of principals nonetheless recognise that they will need to become more responsive over the next few years, and almost three quarters expect to give greater priority to employer links.[35]

Case study 5: West Nottinghamshire College – Learn@Work

West Nottinghamshire College has set up a dedicated business training service for local small and medium-sized enterprises in ten key employment sectors, including IT, Care, Catering and Call Centres. Under the Learn@Work brand, the service operates from a discrete unit on a local business park, offering distance learning with support from individual tutors available 24 hours a day, 7 days a week.

The College has recruited 70 tutors, mainly specialist trainers, to work with local businesses and support learners. In just over a year, Learn@Work has delivered to 500 local businesses and 2,000 employees. Learning can take place in the workplace, at local learning centres or in the college. Most learning is free to the employer, although a charge is made for courses leading to NVQs and some Learn@Work programmes are able to cover their costs.

So far 120 people have achieved NVQs, learning terminals have been located permanently in 15 companies, and Modern Apprentices have been supported in 210 firms. Retention and achievement on distance learning courses are over 90 per cent. The College has been invited by neighbouring Derbyshire LSC to be a provider in its Employer Training Pilot.

Setting up the service required a big up-front investment by the College, which has set a break-even budget of £1.5 million for the service by 2002/03.

---

34 According to research by the Business Development Network.

35 ECOTEC Research & Consulting Limited, for DfES: survey on the views of a third (133) of college principals, to be published in July 2003.

6.5 Colleges and training providers often have a good understanding of their local community and are committed to meeting its needs. But the current public funding regime for adult training can present barriers. There has been limited practical and financial support to colleges and training providers to build their skills training capability. Employers have not always articulated their needs well. The funding and performance monitoring system can encourage providers to stick to mainstream qualifications, while the audit requirements can discourage innovative, customised responses.

6.6 The *Success for All* programme announced in November 2002[36] introduced reforms to raise quality and effectiveness in colleges and training providers. The main elements for this strategy are:

a. **Meeting needs, improving choice**. New arrangements for reviewing the pattern of post-16 provision in each local Learning and Skills Council (LSC) area to fill gaps, remove duplication and encourage specialisation.

b. **Putting teaching, training and learning at the heart of what we do**. The creation of a new Standards Unit, to develop new teaching and learning materials and promote professional development.

c. **Developing the leaders, teachers, trainers and support staff of the future**. This includes a new focus on professional training for leaders and managers across the LSC-funded sector, with a national leadership college for principals and senior managers.

d. **Developing a framework for quality and success**. The introduction of three year budgets, linked to a performance management framework which rewards success.

6.7 Colleges, the LSC and other partners have already started to implement the reforms, and that momentum must be maintained. But further measures, reflecting the *Success for All* principles, can help colleges and training providers to make their full contribution to meeting the skills challenge.

DEVELOPING SUPPLY TO MEET LOCAL NEEDS AND OFFER WIDER CHOICE

6.8 Local LSCs now have allocations for three years and much greater discretion to deploy those budgets to meet local needs. They are reviewing the pattern of publicly-funded provision. This Strategic Area Review process includes deciding which providers each local LSC will fund. A key factor will be providers' assessment of their own missions. All providers are being asked to look rigorously at their services and decide which ones should be expanded or maintained, as well as those which might need to be scaled back or dropped over the next few years.

---

36 Department for Education and Skills (2002) *Success for All*

6.9 We intend that the reviews will lead to:

  a. More business centres within general further education colleges, with distinct objectives, management and culture.

  b. More 'Business Colleges' – general further education colleges specialising in skills and the needs of the local economy as their core mission.

  c. Specialist units or providers serving regional and sub-regional markets, as well as their own immediate localities.

  d. Some private and voluntary training providers who are currently funded only for training young people being funded to provide training for adults as well.

  e. Collaborative models for colleges and training providers to meet the needs of employers.

6.10 The reviews will consider whether new private and voluntary sector providers should be brought within the scope of LSC funding, in order to fill gaps in the quantity or quality of provision. The aim is to offer a wide choice for employers and for individuals of high-quality, distinctive training programmes. That choice cannot be unfettered. Public funds can only be allocated to providers which can offer high quality, relevant programmes. We are currently putting a lot of effort and resource into building higher and more consistent quality across the LSC-funded sector. That has entailed withdrawing funds from many providers where quality was low or provision unviable. Work has already started on enabling training providers to offer literacy, language and numeracy provision in a flexible funding arrangement.

6.11 Nonetheless, it remains important that those private training providers – both for-profit and voluntary – offering distinctive, high quality programmes which can enhance the range of local learning opportunities should be able to access LSC funds. In each Strategic Area Review, the local LSC should consider whether there are such providers that could usefully be included within the scope of LSC funding. Any provider should be able to apply for funding, against a clear, published statement of the criteria it would need to meet. The Skills for Business Network, Union Learning Representatives and others should draw the LSC's attention to providers they are working with, whom they know to be offering distinctive and high quality provision, for the LSC to consider.

CENTRES OF VOCATIONAL EXCELLENCE AND BUILDING CAPACITY TO SUPPORT EMPLOYER NEEDS

6.12 Centres of Vocational Excellence (CoVEs) are specialist training and educational units within colleges, private training providers or companies which receive extra funding to develop quality provision focusing on meeting employers' skills needs. The LSC is committed to expanding their network to 400 by 2006. There are already over 200 CoVEs in development. Case study 6 gives an example.

Case study 6: CoVE for Construction

The creation of a CoVE in Cambridgeshire is part of a strategy to address skills shortages in the construction industry in the East of England. The Cambridgeshire CoVE in construction is currently running 42 courses offering a range of flexible attendance patterns, as well as a range of programmes tailored to individual employers' needs. Research shows that 77 per cent of employers agree that the right range of training is being offered to suit their business needs.

The CoVE is using a fast-track on-site assessment and training programme, and, as part of a wider strategy for 14-19 year olds, has introduced a construction summer school, which will give pupils an insight into career prospects in the building industry and hands on experience in bricklaying, carpentry and plumbing.

6.13 We will develop the Centre of Vocational Excellence programme in the following three ways, set out below.

6.14 First, regional partnerships, including Regional Development Agencies (RDAs), will further develop their role in ensuring that there are sufficient centres in each region to meet skills priorities. As CoVEs develop, we expect them to move beyond the initial focus on level 3 qualifications to provide wider services to their local or sectoral employers, including level 2, basic skills, and supervisory and management training.

6.15 Second, we will enable the Skills for Business Network to play a greater role in shaping the pattern of CoVEs in their sectors. Since CoVEs are designed to meet the skill needs of identified sectors, it is important that the relevant Sector Skills Council (SSC) is fully involved. Over time, we want the Skills for Business Network to support national CoVE networks, so that individual CoVEs work with those in the same specialism. An example of one such network is the automotive academy, as in case study 7.

Case study 7: Automotive Academy

The automotive industry is working with DTI, the DfES and the LSC to develop a sector academy to address lifelong learning throughout its supply chain. A national hub, located in the West Midlands, will co-ordinate regional networks of CoVEs, linked to higher education and private trainers across the country. The network will provide programmes at different skill levels, supported by best practice materials developed by the hub and endorsed by the industry. The network will co-ordinate training for trainers and help to develop internet-based learning and teaching materials. Pilot activities will begin in October 2003 with a full launch in October 2004.

6.16 Third, we want to develop the capability of colleges and training providers to offer a wider range of support for local businesses. This approach has been applied successfully in higher education for some years through the Higher Education Reach Out to Business and the Community Fund, and subsequently the Higher Education Innovation Fund. The CoVE programme covers some of the same ground in further education by supporting specialist skills and qualifications. But it does not help colleges and other training providers offer the full range of business support. Some colleges and CoVEs already provide that full range themselves, but there is room for many more to do so. A recent report by the Learning and Skills Development Agency[37] examined the scope for such a programme, which will be developed jointly between the Department for Education and Skills (DfES), the LSC and the Department of Trade and Industry (DTI).

REFORMING FUNDING AND PLANNING

6.17 The LSC will reform the funding system for adult learning to increase the flexibility for colleges and other providers to deliver customised services to employers. This will build on the principle of `funding by plan` already identified by the LSC. Colleges and training providers will determine how they use their budgets for adult learning and for business support, based on their knowledge of the local environment and their development plan agreed with the local LSC. In particular:

a. For short customised courses (and possibly some provision leading to units or other outcomes short of full qualifications) providers will receive block funding linked to this plan, rather than according to the current complex formula based on progress against each qualification aim for every individual learner.

b. The LSC will scrap the rules in its formula funding methodology which provide lower funding for courses defined as "dedicated to a single employer". The rule has artificially suppressed the supply of customised provision for employers and created excessive audit burdens.

c. The LSC will simplify the formula approach to funding units of qualifications to pave the way for unitisation within the qualifications framework.

6.18 The LSC consulted on the principles of funding reform in April 2003. It will issue a further consultation document in September. This will deal in more detail with the scope and operation of funding by plan, leading to announcements in January 2004 of changes to be implemented from 2004/05.

6.19 These reforms will work within the wider approach to planning skills priorities by region and sector set out in chapter 7, so that the plans which local LSCs agree with

37 Learning and Skills Development Agency (2003) *Further Supporting Business: research-related support for company development*

each training provider are set within the context of clear regional and sectoral frameworks.

Case study 8: Wiltshire and Swindon LSC

Local collaboration to meet employer, regional and sector needs

Wiltshire and Swindon LSC and the South West RDA identified that the tourism and hospitality sector was in need of upskilling in their area. They jointly funded the Tourism Skills Network Wiltshire to help employers and training providers identify training needs in their area, and the delivery methods required to meet them. 247 employers and 418 employees have participated in the project since it started in April 2002.

A range of approaches have been used:

- A group of Farmstay UK members received quality assurance training in one of their own businesses, at times suitable to the group.

- Bowood House in Wiltshire is open seasonally, from April to October, but once the house is open there is little time to release staff for training. They asked the Tourism Skills Network to help with the problem of delivering First Aid courses. The Network identified a trainer able to offer training immediately before the season started.

- Alternative learning methods are being developed with Farmstay UK, with options for learners to go to a Learning Centre or learn on-line at home.

BUILDING CAPACITY OF TRAINING PROVIDERS

6.20 If colleges and other publicly-funded training providers are to offer responsive, customised support, they must have the capacity and incentives to do so. The *Success for All* strategy is intended to secure this.

Incentives

6.21 All colleges will see a 2 per cent real terms increase in the core unit of funding in 2003/04. Thereafter further increases will depend upon performance, with excellent colleges getting a 3.5 per cent real terms increase in the unit of funding in 2004/05 and 2005/06. Performance will be judged against four headline targets, one of which will be a locally agreed target for strengthening college links with employers. The LSC will monitor the impact of its new arrangements on services to employers, and will publish the results of its first national employer satisfaction survey this summer, which will provide a baseline for future annual surveys.

6.22 Capital funding is also important to help colleges and other training providers offer up-to-date training facilities. There will be a 60 per cent real terms increase in LSC capital budgets by 2005-06 compared with 2002–03.

Support

6.23 We will support colleges and training providers in ensuring that they have sufficient competent, qualified trainers and teachers to deliver good skills training. *Success for All* includes a package of support to increase the attractiveness of employment in further education. In addition:

a. The first eight good practice frameworks for teaching and learning developed by the DfES' Standards Unit will prioritise the areas of construction, Entry to Employment (E2E), business studies, science, health and social care, ICT, maths, and land-based skills.

b. The programme to ensure fully qualified lecturers and trainers by 2010 will also cover staff in work-based providers. Our target is that 90 per cent of full-time and 60 per cent of part-time college lecturers will have a teaching qualification or be enrolled on a course by 2006. Work-based providers will be encouraged to set targets for the qualifications of their staff.

c. A partnership of former National Training Organisations is consulting on the establishment of an SSC covering those working in lifelong learning.

ICT and e-learning

6.24 New technologies can transform the way colleges and training providers deliver their services, through developing their capital infrastructure, providing good interactive content, supporting teacher training, and enhancing the delivery of teaching and assessment. Good progress has been made in the use of ICT in the post-16 sector, through the National Learning Network, Ufi/**learndirect** activities, the report from the Distributed and e-Learning Group to the LSC, and the DfES' post-16 e-learning taskforce report, *Get on with IT*.

6.25 The DfES is developing a national e-learning strategy for consultation in July 2003. Within that, we have developed an action plan jointly with the LSC for post 16 e-learning. Its implementation will be jointly managed between the Department and the LSC, supported by over £200 million invested directly by the LSC over three years. The four priorities will be:

a. **Content:** There will be a new National Learning Network portal so that tutors and learners can carry out a single search across all relevant e-learning resources. A demonstrator portal will be trialled from autumn 2003, allowing users to search across a number of linked repositories of learning and support materials. We will make a major investment in new content to fill gaps in provision, purchasing some learning resources centrally, and providing funding so that teaching staff can develop their own or acquire commercial e-learning materials.

b. **Infrastructure:** Good progress has been made in developing internet connectivity and access to PCs within further education and sixth form colleges. This investment will be maintained, and similar investments offered to adult and community learning providers and specialist colleges. Colleges will be connected to higher speed broadband (to mirror developments within schools).

c. **Staff skills:** We will raise the e-learning skills of teachers and support staff. We will develop e-learning standards, and provide training needs analysis and self-assessment tools. The existing staff development programme will be extended. Technological and other IT and e-learning support services currently provided through Regional Support Centres will be expanded down to local level. Leaders and managers will be given training and support to ensure their organisations can make the best use of the new technologies.

d. **Research and planning:** The three priorities are: to research users' current and future e-learning needs, to establish teaching and learning models to help design e-learning delivery, and to develop standards for delivery platforms and content to meet technical and teaching requirements.

FUNDING AND FEES

6.26 Public funding will continue to be a major component of the resources available for skills training. But employers and individuals have always been expected to contribute as well because of the benefits they derive. That contribution is reflected in the charging of fees. There is an assumed fee contribution of 25 per cent of basic course costs for further education learners. Adult and community learners on average pay around 40 per cent towards the cost of their courses. A contribution of 50 per cent of basic course costs has been expected from employers receiving specific provision delivered in their workplace.

6.27 In recent years, this fee income has fallen, with colleges choosing to remit the fees that should have been charged to large numbers of students and employers. There are three reasons:

a. Ambitious Government targets for growth in publicly-funded learning were reflected in the funding system in such a way that it became rational for a college to waive fee contributions if that helped to maximise its student enrolments.

b. Colleges which do try to charge the assumed fees fear being undercut by other publicly-funded providers who do not charge the fees.

c. Worries that fees might discourage involvement by the disadvantaged and economically inactive.

6.28 But the failure to collect fees has significantly reduced what each provider can spend on delivering skills training. The risk is that their income falls to a level insufficient to deliver good quality courses. The Government believes that this position has to be addressed. We have already increased funding significantly for the next three years. Going beyond that to make up the fees shortfall by increasing Government funding further is not affordable within current budgets. Nor is it equitable, given the substantial benefits which learners and employers derive from higher skills and qualifications.

6.29 As argued in chapter 4, we believe it is right to prioritise the use of public funds to help those adults who have no qualifications, to support them in achieving a full level 2 qualification, which represents a platform of employability skills. So adults taking up that entitlement will be offered free tuition with no fees charged. We will also maintain the existing national fee remission arrangements for other priority groups such as those on income-related benefits. The consequence of prioritising some groups of learners is that other learners who have already achieved qualifications at level 3 or above and are seeking further qualifications at the same or lower levels will be expected to pay higher fees.

6.30 We therefore intend to introduce a new national framework for the setting of fees in further education. We and the LSC will consult separately on the best approach involving the Association of Colleges, the Association of Learning Providers and others. The approach we expect to apply is to set, as part of the 'funding by plan' approach described in paragraph 6.17 above, an aggregate income target for each college and training provider. We intend to phase in this approach from 2004/05.

6.31 That target would cover income earned both from employers and from learners through fees. Those fees would be set in the light of the national priorities indicated in chapter 1, but otherwise each provider would continue to determine its own fee schedule. The aim is to leave each college and training provider with maximum discretion to set fees in the light of local circumstances, while avoiding any need for data and audit checks at the level of the individual learner, but against a strong national framework of expectations about the types of learners who can properly be expected to contribute more towards the costs of their learning. As part of that further work, we will need to clarify the contributions expected from employers for different forms of training.

CUTTING BUREAUCRACY

6.32 Colleges and training providers feel that the funding system does not always help them meet employer and learner needs. This chapter has set out a number of changes to tackle specific problems. But we need a wider simplification of funding and the associated audit arrangements for colleges, as identified by the Bureaucracy Taskforce's first report, *Trust in the Future* (2002). The Taskforce will produce a further report on simplification of funding for work-based learning and other training providers. The DfES and LSC are introducing a new standing group, chaired by Sir Andrew Foster, to scrutinise all policies and procedures, to remove all unnecessary red-tape.

6.33 In April the LSC consulted on what further changes might be desirable to simplify funding. There are several areas where early change could bring significant benefits, including making more effective use of management information and changing the procedures for clawing back funds from colleges which undershoot their targets. These changes would be introduced by the LSC following consultation. Changes would be piloted in 2004/05 and introduced nationally in 2005/06.

Chapter 7

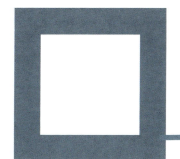

Partnerships for Delivery

SUMMARY OF THIS CHAPTER

7.1 Successful delivery of this Skills Strategy will depend on stronger partnerships between those who deliver services. The Government will take the lead by bringing departments and agencies with responsibility for skills and business support together nationally. Regionally and locally, organisations which help employers to meet their demand for skills must work more effectively with those who plan and fund courses.

7.2 We will:

a. Build a new Skills Alliance, which will ensure that Government departments and agencies work together to implement the Skills Strategy.

b. Organise joint working at regional and local level between the Skills for Business Network, the Regional Development Agencies, the Learning and Skills Council, the Small Business Service and Jobcentre Plus. The form such collaboration takes will vary. So we will invite the Regional Development Agency in each region, working with its partners, to put forward their own proposals for joint working.

c. Ensure cross-Government collaboration in three specific areas relevant to skills:

   i) Between the Department for Education and Skills and the Department of Trade and Industry in carrying forward the Innovation Review.

ii) Between the Department for Education and Skills and the Department for Work and Pensions in joining up the work of Jobcentre Plus and the Learning and Skills Council.

iii) Between the Department for Education and Skills and the Home Office in strengthening skills and training in prisons.

d. Ensure that the Government leads by example as a major employer, with departments investing in skills to improve public services.

7.3 Delivering this strategy is not just about meeting our national needs. It also supports the work we are doing with our European partners to tackle the challenges of skills and mobility across the European Union. The actions in this strategy will be our contribution to that agenda, and the successful delivery of these proposals will enable us to share best practice across Europe.

THE SKILLS ALLIANCE

7.4 Many of the reforms set out in this strategy are about getting different parts of the system to operate more effectively in pursuing shared objectives. This is why we will form a new Skills Alliance – a new social partnership for skills – to bring together key economic and delivery partners who will work with the Government to drive forward the Skills Strategy delivery plan.

7.5 The Skills Alliance will comprise the key departments (the Department for Education and Skills, Department of Trade and Industry, Department for Work and Pensions, and the Treasury), the economic partners (the CBI, Trades Union Congress (TUC) and Small Business Council), and the key delivery agencies. Within the Skills Alliance, the Delivery Partners group will focus on effective implementation of the strategy. The Skills Alliance will meet regularly, under the leadership of the Secretary of State for Education and Skills and the Secretary of State for Trade and Industry. The Alliance will:

a. Engage employers, trade unions and their representative organisations in taking forward the strategy.

b. Monitor progress in implementing the strategy.

c. Advise the Government on ways of enhancing the design and effectiveness of the Skills Strategy.

d. Ensure collaboration between the key agencies in delivering the shared objectives on skills and business support through the new regional structures.

e. Report annually on progress.

7.6   The Sector Skills Councils (SSCs) need to be major contributors at regional as well as national level. We have described the role we want them to play in chapter 3.

7.7   Beyond that, it is vital to have effective regional and local partnerships, with clear roles and responsibilities. There is a strong regional dimension to the skills problem. Variations in the UK regions' skills composition are a major factor in explaining regional variations in productivity. The provision of learning opportunities must respond to each region's skills needs. Our aim is to ensure maximum flexibility and discretion at the regional and local level to innovate, respond to local conditions and meet differing consumer demands.

7.8   Recognising this, in July 2001 the Secretaries of State from the Department for Education and Skills (DfES), the Department for Work and Pensions (DWP) and the Department of Trade and Industry (DTI) asked the Regional Development Agencies (RDAs) to take the lead in producing Frameworks for Regional Employment and Skills Action (FRESA). The FRESA is a plan agreed by RDAs and their key partners including the local Learning and Skills Councils, Jobcentre Plus, Local Authorities, Government Offices, the TUC and representatives of employers. They are designed to address the skills and employment needs of employers and individuals in the region. The output of the process is an action plan setting out priorities and describing how the partners will address them. Each region has now produced a first version of its FRESA. These set out for the first time an overall picture of skills and employment issues in a region within an economic, demographic and social context. The box below sets out case studies of RDA activity to support skills.

Case study 9: RDA activity to support skills

South West Regional Development Agency
A3 Workforce Development – the A3 (Awareness, Advice and Action for Skills Development) Programme in Bournemouth, Dorset and Poole is improving the productivity and competitiveness of local businesses by working to improve the skills of the workforce (Workforce Development Programme) and aid graduate employment (Graduates into Business). Between April 2001 and September 2002, 2,835 people have been helped through the Workforce Development Programme with almost 4,000 training opportunities, and 192 graduates have been supported through the Graduates into Business programme.

South East England Development Agency (SEEDA)
SEEDA and partners are developing a workplace basic skills project in every county in the South East. For example, they are working with the 72 National Health Service (NHS) Trusts in the region to provide workplace basic skills programmes. The approach is two pronged attracting people back into learning, and training more basic skills tutors.

SEEDA has worked with e-skills UK Sector Skills Council and leading businesses in the computer software sector to develop after school computer clubs aimed at preventing girls from losing interest in IT in their pre- and early teen years. The clubs provide the opportunity to develop software and web pages linked closely to the pop and fashion industries and are already heavily over subscribed.

East Midlands Development Agency (*emda*)

'Get On With Graduates' matches the skills and aptitudes of recent graduates to the specific requirements of small and medium sized enterprises within the region. *emda* has contributed £280,000 to the scheme that aims to help firms increase productivity and market penetration, whilst encouraging graduates to build a career within the East Midlands. In 2002–03 the scheme placed 227 graduates on the programme against its annual target of 140. The key to the programme is the use of a strong network of local agents who focus on meeting the skills needs of companies, matching the graduates to their requirements.

London Development Agency

In common with all other regions, London has a Framework for Regional Employment and Skills Action (FRESA), which was launched in March 2003. The London FRESA aims to ensure that employment and skills programmes better serve the needs of Londoners and businesses in the capital. It represents the first fully collaborative approach to addressing London's skills shortages. Among the new London FRESA initiatives are the following three 'flagship' programmes:

- NHS pan-London skills escalator to recruit and retain more health care professionals

- Construction skills programme to tackle the severe shortage of skilled staff in the sector

- Basic skills programme to address the urgent need for more teachers of basic skills.

7.9   That gives a good platform on which to build. But there remains concern that the integrating mechanisms are not yet strong enough at regional and local level to ensure the closeness of collaboration that is needed. We do not want to set up new organisations. But the existing organisations must have a framework which drives constructive, creative joint working to link the assessment of economic strategy by region and sector; the skills, business support and labour market services needed to raise productivity; support for employees and employers to promote investment in skills; and the allocation of funds to training providers.

7.10 We will therefore invite the RDA in each region to agree with its partners what structure will best deliver a better skilled workforce to support the achievement of the Regional Economic Strategy. The partners are the Regional Development Agency, the local Learning and Skills Councils, the Small Business Service, Jobcentre Plus and the Sector Skills Development Agency, supported by the relevant Government Office. They will consult with other partners including Connexions, Local Authorities, Ufi/**learndirect**, Local Strategic Partnerships, and representatives of employers and employees. The partners in each region will be asked to present their agreed proposals by the end of 2003.

7.11 Our basic model for the broad relationships is shown in chart 1 in chapter 1. The primary roles of each organisation are shown in table 5 below. Beyond that, we will not prescribe a particular form of partnership in the regions. We will welcome innovative proposals covering planning, governance and funding, with a view to securing clear lines of accountability and effective action without creating new organisations. Collaboration needs to cover activities funded both by national government and through European funds.

7.12 In developing this approach, we recognise that RDAs must continue to improve their capacity to deliver. That includes reforming their performance management structure to reflect this increased focus on supporting regional skills development.

Table 5: National, regional and local roles

Learning and Skills Council

- At national level, sets strategic policy framework for operation of local LSC planning and funding; and works with Skills for Business Network on sector skills agreements

- At regional level, participates in regional skills partnership, so that the conclusions can feed through to local delivery

- At local level, plans and funds the supply of training, skills and qualifications, in the light of sectoral and regional skill needs, in order to meet local needs

Regional Development Agency

- Develops Regional Economic Strategy to meet employer needs and regional priorities

- Funds regional regeneration and economic development programmes

- Co-ordinates regional skills partnership, to ensure the regional partners agree skills and business support needs to meet the Regional Economic Strategy

Sector Skills Development Agency

- Manages setting up, co-ordination and development of Skills for Business Network, and acts as ambassador for the network

- Co-ordinates across the Skills for Business Network the development of good skills and productivity analysis, and the development of the sector skills agreement model

- Through the regional network ensures that the views and interests of Sector Skills Councils are represented to regional partners

Sector Skills Councils – Skills for Business Network

- Define occupational standards for skills for each sector, as a basis for designing qualifications and courses

- Act as national lead source of expertise on skills and productivity trends, skills needs and labour market analysis for each sector

- Develop skills agreement where appropriate for their sector

- Work with the LSC on designing national skills programmes

- Results feed into regional skills partnerships to shape local training supply

Small Business Service

- At national level, sets framework for performance management of Business Link services

- At regional level, participates in skills partnership to agree regional objectives for business support services which best serve Regional Economic Strategy

Jobcentre Plus

- At national level, sets framework for performance management of Jobcentre Plus local operations, including skills/training

- At regional level, participates in skills partnership to agree objectives for Jobcentre Plus activities to support Regional Economic Strategy and its skills needs

7.13 The development of regional collaboration can draw on two current pilots. We are piloting new partnerships between RDAs and local LSCs in four regions: the North West, North East, Eastern region and the South East. The pilots aim to increase employer demand for skills and the responsiveness of provision to business needs, and to equip more adults with the skills, competences, knowledge and understanding which employers need, thereby raising productivity and economic competitiveness.

7.14 Local LSC and RDA partnerships are developing approaches to joint working regionally, in particular by testing ways of pooling their budgets for adult learning and skills activities and using funds in ways which will enhance flexibility and responsiveness at a regional level. The partnerships will also identify barriers to joint working and seek to address those.

7.15 Additionally, the Small Business Service has introduced three pilots to improve regional co-ordination and management of business support. The pilots, which involve RDA management of Business Link contracts for their regions, are operating in the North West, East Midlands and West Midlands. They are testing different ways of integrating Business Link delivery with the wider range of regional business support. They will also seek to ensure that regional business support services reflect the objectives of Regional Economic Strategies.

7.16 The evaluation of both programmes, particularly in the North West which is operating both pilots, will generate important lessons on the ways in which RDAs can work more effectively with local LSCs and Business Links.

7.17 The Core Cities initiative has identified skills and education as a fundamental driver in developing a knowledge-driven economy, equipping us to attract international and inward investment. Individual Core Cities are developing new means to link investment in skills to building city competitiveness. They propose to build on this to develop a generic model for city learning.

BUILDING LEARNING COMMUNITIES

7.18 We are keen to develop the concept of learning communities. The regional skills partnerships described above would focus on linking skills, business support and economic development in a concerted drive to raise regional and local productivity and growth. But there is a different form of local partnership which we also need to promote – the capability of communities to develop their collective base of skills and learning as learning communities.

7.19 In many disadvantaged areas, low community expectations and aspirations are a significant factor holding back the prospects for economic and social development. That is reinforced by low skills, low achievement and early drop out by young people from education, and an assumption that learning and skills are not relevant to people's lives once they have left school. Several RDAs and their partners have identified the need to build community aspirations as a major factor in achieving their goals for economic regeneration and development, and have reflected this in their FRESAs.

7.20 The importance of skills in tackling community disadvantage has long been recognised. Skills and learning are a major element of the Government's Neighbourhood Renewal Programme, because they can help break the cycle of deprivation, underachievement and worklessness. In some communities, that cycle is being perpetuated from one generation to the next. By raising skills and encouraging learning, parents, grandparents, carers and wider family are better placed to help their children succeed at school; the role and capacity of community leaders can be strengthened; more people can gain sustainable, rewarding jobs or move into self-employment; and more people can get the confidence and know-how to set up and run social enterprises, or take part in voluntary activity.

7.21 One approach would be to encourage individuals, families and employers to see themselves as members of the learning community, with membership bringing locally determined benefits. Those might include regular information about local learning opportunities, taster courses and invitations to family learning events. The aim would be to give membership some of the status and value associated with being a member of a leisure or sports club.

7.22 By encouraging that connectivity of learning, linking schools, colleges and the wide range of skills development and informal learning, different members within a community can both contribute to, and be helped by, the learning and skills of others. That could be a powerful way of tackling inequality, and helping disadvantaged communities to help themselves.

7.23 Local Strategic Partnerships have been formed in all parts of the country as a way of linking up all those activities and services which can in combination help to tackle the range of problems in a community. In the 88 most deprived parts of the country, the partnerships are the route for funding neighbourhood renewal activities. Within Local Strategic Partnership areas there are local learning partnerships specifically focused on bringing together the parties who can promote learning and skills to support community development. In order to narrow the gap between our poorest neighbourhoods and the rest, we must invest in supporting those involved in delivery. *The Learning Curve* – the learning and development strategy for neighbourhood renewal launched in October 2002 – sets out how this can be done. Union Learning Representatives may have a role, building on their work to help the low skilled gain access to training.

7.24 Within the framework now set by this Skills Strategy, we want to work with the existing Local Strategic Partnerships to renew the drive to build learning communities, and form a much stronger link to the regional economic agenda led by the RDAs. This should cover those activities supported by European Structural Funds.

7.25 We envisage trialling the concept initially in areas of long term systemic low aspirations. We will ask the Government Office in each region to support RDAs, local LSCs and Local Strategic Partnerships in their region to define and nominate suitable areas. By building learning communities, we can develop the capacity of disadvantaged areas to create a better future for themselves. The objective is to show

how we can link up the activities and budgets which currently support the RDA role in helping all communities in their region gain access to economic opportunities, the LSC role in widening participation in learning, and the Local Strategic Partnership role in tackling the connected root causes of community disadvantage. We expect plans to promote learning communities to be included in the work of the regional skills partnerships set out above.

Case study 10: Building learning communities: Peepul Centre

The Peepul Centre in Belgrave, Leicester, aims to help local people to become the change agents in their own communities. It has raised £14.4 million to create a purpose-built facility offering the services required to meet local needs. It will be fully operational by the end of 2004.

The development of the centre is working with the ethos of community-led regeneration in partnership with such agencies as the local Learning and Skills Council, Leicester College, De Montfort and Leicester Universities, Leicester City Council, Business Link and the East Midlands Development Agency. The Centre will support individuals within various communities including Asian, African and White communities, young people, elders and women to help them realise their potential and to build a sustainable community through:

- Engaging reluctant learners

- Expanding participation in learning

- Supporting community enterprise

- Building links with employers

Individuals will be helped to meet their aspirations through formal learning, shadowing, work experience and mentoring to ensure that local people are able to apply for jobs created through this and other regeneration projects. The project will foster and embed a culture of learning so that, over time, local communities will be able to take the lead in driving sustainable prosperity.

SKILLS REFORM ACROSS EDUCATION, BUSINESS SUPPORT AND WELFARE TO WORK

7.26 The Skills Strategy is one part of the Government's wider reform agenda for education and training. Annex 1 shows how the DfES' strategies relate to each other, and the key skills elements of the reforms in each sector, together with initiatives by other departments which support the skills agenda.

Skills and Productivity Partnerships across Government: Innovation, the Labour Market and the Prison Service

7.27 There are three further areas where Government departments and agencies will work more closely together – innovation, labour markets, and training in prisons.

Skills and Innovation: The DTI Innovation Review and Skills

7.28 Throughout this White Paper we have emphasised the relationship between skills, innovation and enterprise in raising productivity. The DTI will publish its strategy and action plan for improving the UK's performance as an innovator later this year, emphasising how this can also help close the productivity gap.

7.29 New knowledge and information are critical to innovation. Such knowledge may be self-generated or come from external sources, such as university research. Many firms have their own dedicated research or development units, or routinely develop new ideas through their mainstream operations. But firms need their own workforces to have the skills to initiate new ideas and working methods in-house or to work with external partners to secure them.

7.30 Training and education enable firms to absorb and apply new knowledge. Acquisition of new research from universities or elsewhere will not in itself drive innovation. Firms also need to be able to act on that knowledge to develop new products or services.

7.31 The review of DTI Business Support has been completed, and is now being implemented to provide a more coherent set of fewer, but more focused, business support products. All new products take account of the underlying principles of the Skills Strategy during their development and, where applicable, will measure their impact on the demand for skills. Some of these new products have already been launched, with the remainder to be launched in 2004/05.

Skills and the Labour Market: DWP and Jobcentre Plus

7.32 The second area in which we intend to develop a much stronger partnership is between DfES, DWP, LSC and Jobcentre Plus.

7.33 Jobcentre Plus' priority, in supporting benefit claimants who are seeking work, is to help them get a job as quickly as possible. The evidence suggests that that 'work first' principle is the most effective way of helping claimants, and that postponing entry to a job in order to train can be counter-productive. But at the same time, there is increasing recognition that for people with low or no skills, we need to focus progressively on encouraging sustainable employment. That is more likely to happen where jobseekers have skills, and the jobs they gain offer continuing training.

7.34 The proportion of jobs in the economy which require higher level skills and qualifications is growing, and the proportion requiring low or no qualifications is shrinking.[38] While overall employment rates, especially for the higher skilled, are rising, those of people with

---

38 See chart 4 and paragraph 15 in DfES (2003) *Skills Strategy and Progress Report: Underlying Evidence*

no qualifications have fallen steadily: only about half of people of working age without qualifications are in employment. That has profound implications, not just for young people and those already in work, but also for those seeking work. Those who have skills and qualifications are more likely to get, and keep, jobs than those without. At the same time, those without skills are most likely to move onto inactive benefits, especially incapacity benefit, and to become detached from the labour market. About 40 per cent of those on incapacity benefits have no qualifications. This must powerfully influence the way in which we shape our approach to skills and the labour market over the medium term, so that we offer the best support to those who will otherwise face the greatest struggle in finding sustainable, rewarding employment.

7.35   Jobcentre Plus already plays a significant role in developing the skills and employability of the workforce. Alongside the LSC, it is a major funding body for adult learning, through programmes such as the New Deals, and Work Based Learning for Adults. This provision is focused on tackling the skills needs and other barriers that make it more difficult for some individuals to find work. In many cases, this provision is less about securing qualifications than about acquiring the skills needed to get started in the workplace, effective job-search skills, and preparation relevant to specific local jobs.

7.36   In the 'Ambition' initiatives, Jobcentre Plus and the National Employment Panel involve employers from specific sectors in the design of training and work experience. They use employers' recruitment requirements to define programme content and the basic standard of readiness for a job. By meeting these requirements, the Ambition programmes can open up better, more sustainable jobs and new career opportunities for jobseekers and unemployed people. They also offer a premier service to employers to enable them to improve productivity and competitiveness.

7.37   Jobcentre Plus contributes to the *Skills for Life* strategy by screening welfare claimants for basic skills gaps and providing help to improve basic skills where needed. We intend from 2004 to:

   a.   Extend screening to all new inactive benefit claimants.

   b.   Implement nationally a short screening test for Jobseekers Allowance claimants.

   c.   Provide incentive payments for those who take up basic skills training.

   d.   Use existing powers under the Jobseekers Act to compel claimants to undertake assessment of their basic skills needs.

   e.   Run further pilots of mandatory training on a larger scale.

7.38   Building on these principles, and the good progress made so far, we will develop the DWP and DfES target and resource allocation structures to support the shared objectives. DWP has a new target to raise the employment rate of the lowest qualified, and is revising the Jobcentre Plus target structure to support this. Our longer term goal is to strengthen the links between placing people in jobs and supporting claimants in gaining skills for sustainable employment, as well as helping those on inactive benefits (some of whom have been out of the labour market for a long time) to develop their job-related skills and qualifications where this provides a route out of benefit dependency. It is important to examine carefully the best way of putting these stronger links into operation. We are asking the National Employment Panel[39] to review how best to do this, including looking at the implications for the target and resource allocation structure, and recommend a way forward by the end of 2003, with a view to beginning implementation from 2004-05.

7.39   Meanwhile, there is much that Jobcentre Plus and LSC can do to work together in providing a better service for individuals and employers. There is already some excellent practice at regional and local level. A series of joint pilots have recently been undertaken by the National Employment Panel to identify how collaboration can be strengthened. And the current pilots which bring together RDA and LSC activities and funds for adult skills and business support are providing a new impetus for collaboration with Jobcentre Plus in pursuing agreed objectives.

7.40   We want to encourage this good practice across the whole LSC and Jobcentre Plus networks in England. The main elements are:

a.   Jobcentre Plus staff will be encouraged to consider the role that training could play in helping inactive benefit claimants prepare for return to the labour market. Customers will be informed of their entitlements to undertake learning, as well as their benefit responsibilities, and offered a referral to further information, advice and guidance on learning, if it seems appropriate. We believe there is a strong case for doing more to ensure that benefit claimants who have been out of the labour market for long periods can access work-based skills. We will ask the National Employment Panel, as part of the review referred to above, to look at the evidence and policy options. Through Sir Roy Gardner (who is a member of the National Employment Panel as well as Chair of the Modern Apprenticeship Task Force), we will also link in the part that Modern Apprenticeships could play in helping benefit claimants.

b.   Jobcentre Plus is a member of each local Information, Advice and Guidance (IAG) partnership. Through local framework agreements, every IAG partnership will ensure that Jobcentre Plus staff are fully briefed on the services other IAG partners can offer, so that they can signpost clients to appropriate help. Jobcentre Plus also has a role in helping these IAG providers to provide a relevant and robust service by keeping them aware of relevant labour market information, and of Jobcentre Plus services and programmes.

39 The Panel is chaired by Sandy Leitch, and reports on skills-related issues jointly to DWP, DfES, and Treasury

c.   IAG partnerships' services will include support in cases where claimants have started a training programme when they take up jobs, to help them receive advice on how they might complete their studies – either part-time, or through their new employer.

d.   Local LSCs and Jobcentre Plus will work together in each local area to improve integration of services for claimants and employers by:

   i)   Creating progression routes from New Deal and other programmes for jobless people into work with learning.

   ii) Joint marketing to, and integrated services for, employers, delivering coherent packages of recruitment and training support to employers. This includes working with employers and Sector Skills Councils in joint delivery of sectoral initiatives.

   iii) Improving the analysis and use of labour market information to help the LSC and Jobcentre Plus staff provide guidance on labour market trends. This will help Jobcentre Plus staff to signal local skills needs and shortages to clients, and to keep the local LSC informed about the pattern of skills needs and gaps identified by local employers.

7.41   We especially want to provide better support for women returning to the labour market after a period bringing up children or caring for dependants. Many of them have a valuable range of skills to offer. But they may lack confidence in knowing how best to move back into employment, and feel that they need to update their previous skills and knowledge, or acquire new skills and qualifications in order to move into new careers. Women returners will be helped by other reforms in this strategy, including the new learner entitlement for those without qualifications, better learner support, and better IAG. From April 2004, DWP will pilot a work search premium, offering an additional £20 per week for lone parents who have been on Income Support for more than a year and who are actively seeking work, rising to £40 per week when the lone parent starts working more than 16 hours per week.

7.42   For lone parents on benefit, Jobcentre Plus and the LSC can play a vital role in making claimants aware of what is available by way of work-focused training, encouraging them to take up such training and achieve new qualifications to support their rapid return to, and effective performance in, the labour market, and encouraging them to consider work that offers opportunities for progression. We will build this into the review by the National Employment Panel referred to above, to signal the priority we attach to helping this group. But we will also treat it as a matter of good practice to be strongly encouraged in the short term as well.

7.43 Jobcentre Plus currently holds a budget of over £500 million to purchase training for claimants who need it. This supports, for example, training in basic skills, short job-focused training, and training under the New Deals. Jobcentre Plus contracts for that training from a wide range of providers, over one-third of which are also LSC funded. This operates separately from the mainstream LSC planning and funding of training for adults. Jobcentre Plus works with the LSC on quality issues, for example, through a joint commitment to *Getting Better Delivery*, the cross-Government guidance on working with learning providers released in May 2003. In the longer term, we want to converge these approaches so that we can take a consistent approach to:

a. Identifying and assessing providers which can offer high quality training to meet client needs.

b. Contracting with providers.

c. Raising quality and standards across all providers, on the principles set out in the *Success for All* programme.

d. Joining funding streams in order to improve outcomes for individuals and employers, and remove obstacles to progression for learners.

7.44 To carry forward the developments described above, we will take the following steps:

a. The Chief Executives of the LSC and Jobcentre Plus will issue guidance to their respective networks on what has been learnt from the pilots undertaken by the National Employment Panel, and how it can be applied across the country. They will systematically publicise to their respective networks examples of the benefits to individuals and employers of successful collaboration that has improved labour market performance.

b. Each regional skills partnership will be asked to consider specifically what regional arrangements will best promote collaboration between the LSC, Jobcentre Plus and other partners in improving services for benefit claimants and employers seeking to fill vacancies. As set out above, we are asking the RDA in each region to lead these discussions. It will be for the partners in each region to decide for themselves what structure to propose, drawing on their experience of developing Frameworks for Regional Employment and Skills Action (FRESA) and the setting up of the pilot programmes to pool RDA and LSC funds for adult skills.

7.45 Both LSC and Jobcentre Plus play an important role in easing the shock to local labour markets caused by major redundancies. The Rapid Response Service in Jobcentre Plus works with local LSCs to assess the impact of a redundancy and, where there are likely to be significant effects, sets in place a tailored solution for the clients, employer and the local economy. People often need help to adapt to new conditions in the labour market, and the Rapid Response Service package where appropriate includes tailored training to help those being made redundant to re-skill and take alternative work. This commitment will be reinforced, so that training will normally be offered as part of the package of interventions for future large-scale redundancies.

Case study 11: Government Response to Redundancies: the North East

Due to restructuring following a downturn in local manufacturing, six companies in a business park in the North East announced 462 job losses to be realised from April to December 2002. The Rapid Response Service intervened because it was clear that the redundancies would have a significant impact on the local labour market.

The Rapid Response Service set up a partnership, bringing together Jobcentre Plus with the local LSC, Business Link and the Regional Development Agency. Through this partnership, a co-ordinated range of assistance was offered:

- The Rapid Response Service offered help to identify individuals' transferable skills and re-training needs, funding for additional training, and early access to a range of standard Jobcentre Plus provision (eg, Work Based Learning for Adults)

- Benefits processing staff offered on-site assistance and advice

- A series of on-site redundancy roadshows, which included local training providers and colleges, who explained options available to the affected workforce

- Business Link offered advice to people considering establishing their own businesses, including business planning and accessing funding as well as training

- The local LSC offered a range of learning to workers affected by the redundancies

---

Prison and Probation Services

7.46 We want stronger collaborative working in the training of offenders. Seven in ten of those convicted of crimes lack even basic skills. Even more lack the wider skills and qualifications required in the jobs market. With better skills, they would have a better chance of getting a job, reducing the likelihood of re-offending.

7.47 So the principles set out in this White Paper must apply to young and adult offenders, serving prison and community sentences. Our goal, as set out in *Improving Offenders' Learning and Skills* (Home Office, 2003), is

"that offenders, according to need, should have access to education and training, both in prisons and in the community, which will enable them to gain the qualifications they need to hold down a job and have a positive role in society, and that the content and quality of learning programmes in prisons, and the qualifications to which these lead, are the same as comparable provision in the community".

7.48 Education and training for prisoners has been improved in recent years. Since 2001, such work has been co-ordinated by the Prisoners' Learning and Skills Unit and funding has risen from £72 million in 2002–03 to £137 million by 2005–06. As a result, 41,000 prisoners achieved basic skills qualifications in 2002–03 alone. Building on that, we will:

a. Provide further opportunities for prisoners to improve their basic skills in literacy and numeracy as part of the *Skills for Life* programme, and to achieve more work-related qualifications.

b. Increase opportunities for prisoners to learn how to use computers and to learn interactively so that prison provision resembles more closely that in the community. This will build on pilot schemes currently underway with Ufi/**learndirect**.

c. Enhance information, advice and guidance services in prisons, offering advice on skills and jobs. Some prisons already have access to the Worktrain internet portal, with information on jobs and training, and the Job Point database.

d. Through the Prison Service Custody to Work initiative, help offenders get better employment, training and accommodation on release. In 2003–04, our target is 31,500 ex-offenders getting jobs or training.

7.49 We will also strengthen the partnership between the Prison Service, the National Probation Service and the LSC, to improve basic skills and other learning opportunities for offenders in the community, including those leaving custody. The new Offenders' Learning and Skills Unit[40] will co-ordinate this new framework, which should be in place by April 2004.

LEADING BY EXAMPLE: THE GOVERNMENT AS EMPLOYER

7.50 Public services, just as much as private businesses, need to be well managed and effective. So they too must invest in the skills of their staff, to raise the productivity of the public service. The Government is a major employer in its own right. There are over 500,000 civil servants directly employed by Government departments and their agencies.

7.51 There are many examples of good practice by Government departments and the public sector in skills and training, as illustrated in annex 4. But there is a great deal more to do to achieve the Government's objectives for public service reform.

7.52 We are taking the following approach:

a. All Government departments are being asked to provide skills development plans by April 2004. These will identify their future skills needs to achieve organisational objectives, assess their current skills baseline, and specify the action to be taken. That includes action to meet the various Government skills priorities including level 2 qualifications, Modern Apprenticeships and Foundation Degrees. This is a model which has already been applied for basic skills, and has achieved substantial impact.

40 The new name for the former Prisoners' Learning and Skills Unit to reflect the fact that it will work with the Probation Service as well as the Prison Service.

b. Progress on the delivery of skills development plans will be overseen by the Cabinet Committee on Economic Affairs, Productivity and Competitiveness, chaired by the Chancellor of the Exchequer.

c. Departments will create a framework of study support, including study leave, for those within the priority groups identified in this strategy – particularly those without a full level 2 qualification who want to get one.

d. The DfES is working with the Cabinet Office on proposals for a Sector Skills Council for government which could cover central government. As with other Sector Skills Councils, any such Council would have a role in defining occupational standards, and working with training providers, including the Civil Service College, to ensure the necessary supply of skills to achieve high quality delivery of public services.

7.53 Guidance has been developed in partnership with the Treasury and Office of Government Commerce to support departments who wish to use the procurement process to ensure contractors' staff have access to basic skills opportunities relevant to the effective delivery of their jobs. The guidance informs departments how they can use existing procurement policy and require contractors to commit to minimum basic skills support for their staff.

7.54 Development of skills across the whole public sector is important to meet our ambition of public service reform. The Local Government Sector is one of the largest employers in the country and has the potential to support the Government's commitment to lead by example. We therefore welcome the LGA's commitment to developing the skills of its own workforce and in particular those with lower level skills.

SUPPORTING EUROPEAN ACTION ON SKILLS
Skills and the Lisbon Agenda

7.55 European Heads of Government agreed, in 2000, the ambitious Lisbon agenda to promote economic reform in Europe to create the conditions for full employment by the year 2010:

> "to become the most competitive and dynamic knowledge-based economy in the world, capable of sustainable economic growth with more and better jobs and greater social cohesion" *European Union strategic goal, 2000*

7.56 Achieving our Lisbon employment targets will not be easy. It will take concerted effort across Government and across the European Union to drive forward the process of economic reform. Developing the skills and lifelong learning agenda is an essential component of our response to the Lisbon challenges. This strategy underpins our efforts to tackle the skills gaps which undermine our economic performance. We want the UK to be an example of good practice which other EU member states can follow, and we want to learn from good practice elsewhere. We are committed to playing our full part in achieving a step change across Europe in skills and training policy.

7.57 This section sets out the synergies between this national strategy and action at the European level.

The European Employment Strategy

7.58 The European Employment Strategy (EES) is designed to be the main tool to give direction to, and ensure co-ordination of, the employment policy priorities to which Member States should subscribe at EU level. Heads of State and Government have agreed on a framework for action based on the commitment from Member States to establish a set of common objectives and targets for employment policy.

7.59 In common with all other EU member states, the UK has agreed to develop its skills policies and improve its educational and training systems to better equip workers with the skills they need to participate in today's labour market; and to encourage lifelong learning. In particular, we have agreed to:

a. Provide appropriate guidance in the context of initial training and lifelong learning.

b. Modernise and ensure the greater effectiveness of apprenticeship systems and in-work training.

c. Reduce youth and adult illiteracy.

d. Promote better access to lifelong learning by adults.

e. Emphasise skills that enhance geographical and sectoral mobility (such as language learning).

f. Promote e-learning for all citizens.

7.60 The plans and reforms set out in this strategy will help us to improve our delivery in these areas. We will report progress on implementation in the regular National Action Plans on Employment we submit to the European Commission, and share good practice with others through the associated peer review process.

Skills and Mobility Action Plan

7.61 In February 2002, the European Commission published its Action Plan on Skills and Mobility, implementing the recommendations of the European Skills and Mobility Taskforce. This details particular areas where an additional emphasis is needed at European level to ensure we develop a labour force which has the necessary skills as well as the capacity to adapt and acquire new knowledge throughout their working lives.

7.62 In particular, we are committed to:

a. Pushing forward work to simplify and extend the European regime on mutual recognition of professional qualifications.

b. Playing our full part in the Education objectives process, which sets out specific actions and benchmarks for the improvements in skills and training needed to support the Lisbon employability agenda.

c. Reforming EU skills-related spending programmes such as SOCRATES and LEONARDO to ensure they focus fully on the Lisbon agenda.

d. Working towards greater European recognition of informal and non-formal learning.

e. Developing an EU framework to ensure transparency and better mutual recognition of vocational qualifications.

f. Playing an active role in the European Year of Education through Sport.

The European Social Fund

7.63 The European Social Fund, together with national funds, has played an important role in supporting our training actions to implement the European Employment Strategy. The future of the European Social Fund beyond 2006 is under discussion. The Government's consultation paper *A Modern Regional Policy for the United Kingdom* (March 2003) sets out a vision for the way forward, which ensures that skills and employment remain at the heart of regional development.

Chapter 8

Delivering the Strategy

SUMMARY OF THIS CHAPTER

8.1   Our strategy is ambitious and far reaching. It is not about short term initiatives, but an agenda for the long term. Previous chapters have outlined our goals and the activities that will contribute to achieving them. They will require sustained effort over several years. Strategies themselves do not produce change. It is their successful implementation that makes a difference. This chapter sets out how we will implement the strategy to ensure successful delivery.

ACHIEVING DELIVERY

8.2   The new national Skills Alliance will oversee the implementation of the strategy, with regular progress reports against the delivery plan set out below.

8.3   There will be clear targets, and indicators to track progress towards the targets. At present, we have a range of relevant Public Service Agreement targets. The Department for Education and Skills targets mostly relate to the achievement of qualifications. Department of Trade and Industry targets link to raising productivity. Department for Work and Pensions targets link to placing people in jobs. We recognise that targets pursued in isolation do not always achieve the best outcomes. We must bring these objectives together towards the shared goal of raising productivity and competitiveness. So one early task for the Skills Alliance will be to agree our shared priority targets which bring together actions to improve productivity and the working of the labour market with actions to improve skills, training and qualifications.

8.4 Successful delivery requires clear lines of accountability. Chapter 7 sets out the broad approach we want to see at regional and local level, and invited the partners in each region to specify for themselves how best to meet those objectives. The Skills Alliance will assess the responses.

COMMUNICATION STRATEGY

8.5 Achieving our objectives depends on persuading large numbers of employers and learners that it is worth taking an interest in skills, training and qualifications. So there must be a communication plan which conveys in clear and simple terms why skills matter and what benefits they bring to individuals and to employers of all sizes.

8.6 There is a lot of experience of what works. The successful 'Gremlins' marketing campaign for adult basic skills, which is now recognised by nine out of ten adults, shows how this can be done. The National Training Awards, organised by UK Skills, show the business gain from investing in skills as well as promoting excellence. Skills competitions and events such as World Skills promote benchmarking of best practice in skills. Adult Learners' Week, organised by the National Institute of Adult Continuing Education (NIACE), provides a platform for a huge range of local activities, with over 3,000 local events this year.

8.7 The challenge is to ensure that the marketing activity relating to skills, training and qualifications undertaken by different agencies works together to achieve a unifying underlying message, consistently delivered, while still having targeted campaigns focused on specific groups.

8.8 We will establish a Strategic Communications Group to develop a communication and marketing plan for skills. The group will include the Department for Education and Skills, Department of Trade and Industry, Learning and Skills Council, Ufi/**learndirect**, Sector Skills Development Agency, Regional Development Agencies, Investors in People UK, Qualifications and Curriculum Authority and UK Skills. The language used to describe different skill levels is not well understood and can cause confusion. We will ask the group to advise the QCA on the development of common descriptions of basic and key skills qualifications, which are clear and straightforward for individuals and employers.

MILESTONES

8.9 The table sets out our initial delivery plan. It does not cover everything in this White Paper, but focuses on the priorities.

Delivery Plan

	Milestone	Date	Owner
Employers	Consider national approach following evaluation of Employer Training Pilots	End 2005	DfES, Treasury
	Employer Guide to Good Training released in each local LSC	December 2004	DfES, LSC
	Leadership and management development programme for SME owner-managers and CEOs launched	December 2003	DfES, IiPUK, SSDA, LSC
	Enhanced business support network:		DTI, DfES
	• First new Business Support products launched	June 2003	
	• Remaining Business Support products launched	April 2004	
	Full Skills for Business Network operational	Summer 2004	DfES, SSDA
	First sector skills agreements developed	End 2004	DfES, DTI, SSDA, LSC
Learners	Entitlement to free learning for first full level 2 qualification:		DfES, LSC
	• Phased introduction begins	Sept 2004	
	• National rollout begins	Sept 2005	
	Pilots of new adult learning grants begin	Sept 2003	DfES, LSC
	Action plan agreed for improving information, advice and guidance services for adults	December 2003	DfES, LSC, Ufi
	Action plan agreed for new approach to funding and planning adult and community learning	December 2003	DfES, LSC

Qualifications	Funding arrangements to reward all providers equally for basic and key skills learning	August 2004	LSC
	Publish Foundation Degree prospectus	Autumn 2003	DfES, Higher Education Funding Council for England
	Review qualifications by sector and identify which best develop the skills foundation for employability in each sector	June 2004	SSDA, Skills for Business Network, QCA
	Publish final report of the working group on 14-19 reforms	July 2004	DfES
	Reform of vocational qualifications for adults: consultation on the programme of work	September 2003	QCA, LSC, SSDA and UK partners
	Implement Modern Apprenticeship quality improvements	From July 2003	LSC
Colleges and Training Providers	Funding reform:		DfES, LSC
	• Funding by plan pathfinders	August 2004	
	• National roll-out of funding by plan	August 2005	
	• New three year funding agreements concluded	July 2006	
	Employer engagement targets for providers agreed	Sept 2003	LSC
	Fees:		
	• National fee framework finalised	August 2005	DfES
	• Income targets agreed with all providers	August 2005	LSC
	400 CoVEs operational	March 2006	DfES, LSC

Partnerships	National Skills Alliance formed	July 2003	DfES
	Innovation Review: • Initial findings • Final report	July 2003 Autumn 2003	DTI
	RDAs, LSC, Small Business Service, Jobcentre Plus put forward proposals for skills partnership structure for each region	December 2003	DfES, DTI
	National Employment Panel completes review of link between skills, training and jobs	December 2003	DWP, DfES
	Strategies for skills in all Government departments	April 2004	Cabinet Office
Delivery	Skills Alliance reviews key performance targets for shared skills/productivity objectives	End 2003	DfES, DTI, DWP
	Communication and marketing plan agreed	December 2003	Strategic Communications Group

Annex 1 Education, Skills and Productivity – the Reform Agenda

The chart shows how our reform strategies connect across the different sectors of the education service.

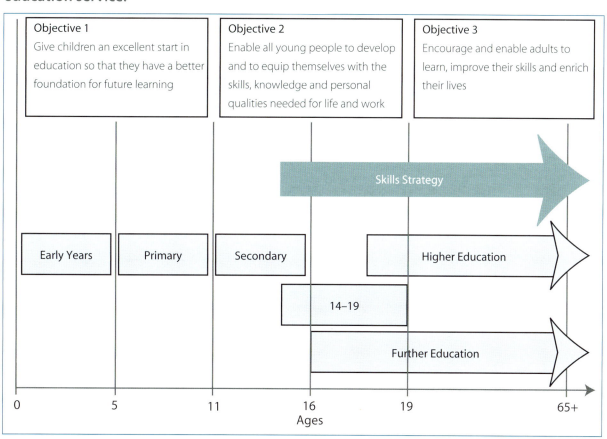

Objective 1	Objective 2	Objective 3
Give children an excellent start in education so that they have a better foundation for future learning	Enable all young people to develop and to equip themselves with the skills, knowledge and personal qualities needed for life and work	Encourage and enable adults to learn, improve their skills and enrich their lives

Skills Strategy

Early Years   Primary   Secondary   Higher Education

14–19

Further Education

0   5   11   16   19   65+

Ages

Education Reforms Supporting the Skills Strategy

Early Years

- Development of foundation skills from the early years – communication, co-operation, creativity

- Provision of high quality, affordable childcare supports early learning and increases parents' opportunities to learn and to work

Primary and Secondary Schools

- Strong emphasis on developing literacy, numeracy and ICT skills as essential foundations for all other learning and subsequent employability

- Focus on developing wider generic skills sought by employers through integration in the curriculum – ability to learn, problem solving, creativity and teamwork

- Close working with employers through work experience placements, work shadowing, involvement of subject specialists, mentoring, governorships, and teacher placements

- 1,400 specialist schools already designated in a range of subject areas (including business and enterprise, and engineering), each with business sponsors who have invested at least £50,000 in the school. Some sponsors play an active part in the school curriculum

- New business-sponsored Academies

- A new entitlement to learn languages throughout Key Stage 2, recognition of the importance of language skills for business and increased employability for individuals

- The range of vocational subjects available at GCSE is being expanded to give secondary-phase pupils more opportunities for applied learning

- Over 40,000 pupils study at college or with a training provider for one or two days a week on specialist vocational courses. More will join this 'increased flexibility' programme from September 2003

14–19 phase	● Reform of the curriculum and qualifications offered to young people aged 14–19
	● Broadening the curriculum at Key Stage 4 to provide more choice of individual pathways better suited to young people's interests and needs. Work-related learning to be available to all, with more young people from 14 onwards spending part of the week in a location other than school pursuing vocational (or specialist) learning
	● Pilots of enterprise learning will increase young people's understanding of the demands of the economy and workplace
	● New GCSEs in vocational subjects available from September 2002
	● From 2004, an entitlement for all young people to develop their communication, number and computer skills up to age 19 until they reach level 2 standard
	● Modern Apprenticeships to be extended so that 28 per cent of 16-21 year olds can enter them by 2004
	● Entry to Employment (E2E) programme for 16–18 year olds
	● Working Group on 14–19 Reform, chaired by Mike Tomlinson, considering longer term reforms to strengthen the vocational offer for young people, what a new unified system of qualifications might look like, and assessment methods that are fit for purpose
Further Education	*Success for All* reforms designed to raise standards across the LSC-funded sector. The reforms cover four elements:
	● Improved responsiveness of provision through LSC Strategic Area Reviews
	● Improving the quality of teaching and learning. Establishment of a new Standards Unit to develop curriculum in each major area
	● New Leadership College for principals and senior managers, and better staff development throughout further education
	● New performance framework for colleges and training providers, including the agreement of three year development plans with a target for improving employer responsiveness for every college

Adult basic skills

- Well over a million learners engaged in literacy, language and numeracy courses between April 2001 and July 2002

- 319,000 adults improved their basic skills from April 2001 to July 2002

- On track to meeting our target of 750,000 adults with better basic skills by 2004 and 1.5 million by 2007

- Over the next three years, we plan to provide over 3 million learning opportunities delivered in ways that suit learners' circumstances

- Learning is being brought to the learner – through local football clubs, by 'mobile' training centres, in the workplace, and through learning 'shops' situated close to main shopping areas

Higher Education

Higher Education White Paper reforms, published January 2003, will develop higher level skills through:

- Expansion of Foundation Degrees to provide strong vocational focus

- Promotion of knowledge transfer from higher education to business, encouraging support for innovation and spin-out companies

- Formation of around 20 Knowledge Exchanges, transferring new ideas from higher education institutions to business, providing advice on their skills implications, and helping businesses develop the skills to make the most of them

- Strong collaboration between DfES and DTI in developing the capacity of universities and higher education colleges to work more closely with employers, through the Higher Education Reach Out to Business and the Community programme and subsequently the Higher Education Innovation Fund

- Development of New Technology Institutes. These are regional consortia, led by HE institutions, working with colleges. They are developing the supply of higher level skills, in ICT and other specialisms, alongside a range of services to small businesses to support adoption of technology

- Richard Lambert's review,[41] announced in the 2002 Pre-Budget Report, is considering ways of strengthening links between business and universities

41 Lambert Review of Business-University collaboration.

Welfare to Work

- Jobcentre Plus aims to deliver an integrated service to all working age benefit recipients, giving them the support they need, while offering help to all to move into the labour market

- The New Deal and other employment programmes help the long-term unemployed gain skills and experience that are relevant to employers, helping them to find work, and helping employers to fill their vacancies

- Two new tax credits – the Child Tax Credit and the Working Families Tax Credit – were introduced from April 2003. These provide an additional £2.7 billion in support for families with children. These tax credits work alongside the national minimum wage to tackle poverty and make work pay

- Better information through the introduction of Job Points, Jobseeker Direct and Jobsbank, connected to third largest jobs database in the world providing information about jobs and training opportunities

Skills for urban and rural renewal

- The Government's programme for Neighbourhood Renewal, led by the Office of the Deputy Prime Minister, is supporting improvement in the most disadvantaged communities, seeking to tackle coherently the multiple causes of deprivation and community decay

- From the outset, the programme has recognised that helping people acquire new skills and knowledge can be a powerful contributor to rebuilding communities. Learning can develop community leadership and new forms of collective social engagement which break down the barriers between individuals, families and groups within a community. Research evidence shows that adult learning can bring social benefits, including greater community tolerance and increased civic participation

- Neighbourhood Learning Centres have featured strongly in the Neighbourhood Renewal programme

- The Learning Skills and Knowledge Programme run by the Department for Environment, Food and Rural Affairs supports the creation and continuing development of rural workforces. The programme is aimed at overcoming cultural and practical obstacles faced by mostly micro-businesses in rural areas, to developing their ambitions

Protecting the rights of workers

- The Sex Discrimination Act, Equal Pay Act, Race Relations Act, and the Disability Discrimination Act provide protection for a range of workers to ensure they have equal access and treatment at work

Annex 2 Aspirations for the Skills Strategy

WHAT SUCCESS WOULD LOOK LIKE FOR AN EMPLOYER

What I want	How will I get it?
I want to recruit as many staff as I need, with the right skills	• Schools, colleges, training providers and universities will do more to prepare young people for the world of work
	• Skills for Business Network and other employer-led organisations will identify what skills employers in each sector need; national and local agencies will work together to ensure those skills are provided
	• Jobcentre Plus helps employers fill their vacancies and helps jobseekers acquire the skills needed by local employers
	• Local working between Jobcentre Plus and local Learning and Skills Councils to deliver coherent recruitment and training packages
	• Employment policies such as flexible working should encourage greater participation in the labour market
Government is helping me build a successful business, recognising that skills are only one means to that end	• Reform of business support services should enable employers to get the information they need; and the business support network will work with a wider range of intermediaries and brokers
	• The business.gov website will be improved to provide access to advice and assessment tools
	• Government departments and agencies will work together to improve the links between skills, employment, innovation and competitiveness

What I want	How will I get it?
I want to decide what training my business needs. I want the Government to help me find it and colleges or training providers to tailor their courses and training packages accordingly	• The Employer Training Pilots give employers greater choice in getting the training they want, with brokerage to help them identify the right programmes for staff with few or no qualifications • We will improve quality and effectiveness in further education colleges and other training providers through our *Success for All* reforms • We will reform the LSC funding system to make it easier for colleges and other training providers to tailor courses to employer needs
I want to see my profits and productivity improve from the investment I am making in skills	• Sector skills agreements link action on skills and productivity • We will make effective diagnostic tools and support services available to make it easier for employers to assess needs and make improvements • We will provide clearer information about bottom line benefits based on best practice and using exemplar companies • We will publish guidance on how to measure and report on human capital management, including investment in skills • We will expand the Investors in People programme
My staff can achieve qualifications in a way that suits their needs and the needs of the business	• We will reform qualifications so that they better reflect business needs, and are more flexible • Reforms to LSC funding will support these changes in offering more flexible qualifications • Employer Training Pilots support training in the workplace
I am getting a joined-up service, in language I can understand, with the different bits of Government working together	• The Skills Alliance will bring together Government departments and national agencies, with representatives of employers and unions • There will be joint targets and joint monitoring of progress • Key regional agencies will work closely together including to deliver business support services

What I want	How will I get it?
The need to invest in skills is widely accepted in this industry, and we work together to achieve it	● Skills for Business Network will support employers working together voluntarily to improve skills and training, in ways that suit the needs of each sector

WHAT SUCCESS WOULD LOOK LIKE FOR AN INDIVIDUAL LEARNER

What I want	How will I get it?
I can see why it is worth investing in skills and qualifications. They will help me get a decent job, to progress and do what I want to do with my life	● We will ensure that agencies work together to give learners the best choice of training opportunities. ● We will encourage more employers to invest in skills, to encourage learners to train at work ● We will introduce a new entitlement to training for those without a skills foundation for employability and extra support with learning costs for those needing most help
I know who to talk to in order to get the advice and information I need	● The Connexions Service will be available nationally for young people aged 13-19 ● We will reform the Information, Advice and Guidance service for adults ● More Union Learning Representatives are being funded to help those in work
I can get help to meet the costs of training	● New entitlement to free full level 2 training for learners who do not already have those qualifications ● More support for level 3 training in areas of sectoral or regional skills priorities ● Better learner support funding, including development of adult learning grants

What I want	How will I get it?
They helped me get back into learning at my own pace, in my own way, without having to go back to school	● Adult and community learning is being reformed, with funding to ensure a continuing range of community, leisure and lifelong learning opportunities ● The work of UK online centres and Ufi/**learndirect** centres is being brought together to give more choices for 'returning to learn' ● Establishment of the Entry to Employment (E2E) programme for 16-18 year olds
My education/ training course is giving me the learning/skills I want	● Reforms to curriculum and qualifications in schools, colleges and training providers, Modern Apprenticeships and higher education are providing more vocational options and give stronger focus on employability ● Wider availability of assessment of existing skills, training to bridge skills gaps, and skills passports ● Reform of qualifications to support learning in units, with a new credit framework ● Local and regional agencies will be working together to ensure skills needs are reflected in training programmes ● More information will be published about the standards of colleges and training providers
I am learning what I need to know, delivered in a way that suits me and my work	● More support for e-learning so learners can study at work and at home ● Wider availability of support to assess existing skills and then train to fill the gaps ● Skills for Business Network identifying key skills for employment in each sector, and reflecting those in qualifications ● Employer Training Pilots offer more support for workplace learning ● We are expanding the network of Union Learning Representatives
I have proved to myself that I can do it – and now I am going to do more	● We will establish clear progression routes, from basic literacy and numeracy and first step programmes, through both general and specialist routes at level 2 and level 3, to Foundation Degrees and higher education ● We will support progression to higher levels of learning, either through the work-based vocational options at levels 4 and 5, or by going into higher education, particularly to study for a Foundation Degree

Annex 3 Sector Productivity and Skills

INDICATOR

BROAD SECTOR	Classification	Employment as % of total economy	Productivity (Gross Value Added per person employed – current prices £000)	% Qualified to NVQ 2 or below	% Qualified to NVQ 3 and above	Proportion of establishments reporting skill gaps – %	Skill gaps as a proportion of employment – %	Skill shortage vacancies as a proportion of employment – %	SECTOR SKILLS COUNCILS whose footprint may include parts of this sector
Agriculture, hunting, forestry and fishing	SSIC 01, 02, 05	1.3	NA	67[1]	30[1]	6.0	3.5	0.6	Lantra
Mining and quarrying	SIC 10, 11, 12, 13, 14	0.4	358.7	33[1]	50[1]	*	*	*	Proskills, Cogent Plus
Manufacturing	SIC 15 to 37	15.7	36.6	54	45	9.2	4.9	0.5	e-skills UK, SEMTA, Proskills, Cogent Plus, Food and Drink, Skillfast–UK
Electricity, gas and water supply	SIC 40, 41	0.8	121.9	38[1]	57[1]	*	*	*	Energy and Utilites Skills
Construction	SIC 45	7.3	36	53	47	4.9	3.5	1.7	Construction Skills, SummitSkills
Wholesale and retail	SIC 50, 51, 52	15.1	24.2	64	35	6.8	4.4	0.5	Automotive Services, Skills for Logistics, Skillsmart, Lantra
Hotels and restaurants	SIC 55	4.4	13.2	65	35	8.4	6.0	0.5	Hospitality, SkillsactiveUK
Transport, storage and communication	SIC 60, 61, 62, 63, 64	7.0	43.3	62	37	6.0	3.4	0.6	Skills for Logistics, GoSkills, e-skills UK
Banking and insurance	SIC 65, 66, 67	4.5	NA	41	58	9.2	3.9	0.5	Financial Services
Real estate, renting and business activities	SIC 70, 71, 72, 73, 74	11.5	34.1	38	61	6.5	3.6	1.7	e-skills UK, Housing and Justice, Property, Construction Skills
Public administration, defence, compulsory social security	SIC 75	6.7	NA	41	59	11.4	4.2	0.2	Justice
Education	SIC 80	8.1	NA	29	70	7.6	1.6	0.4	Lifelong Learning
Health and social work	SIC 85	11.0	NA	43	57	9.2	2.9	0.8	Skills for Health, Social Care
Other services	SIC 90, 91, 92, 93	5.4	24.2	48	51	5.0	3.5	0.9	Skillset, SkillsactiveUK
Whole Economy		**100**	**32.2**	**50**	**50**	**6.9**	**3.9**	**0.8**	

INDICATOR

BROAD SECTOR	Proportion of establishments reporting skill-shortage vacancies - %	Proportion of establishments who funded training in the preceding 12 months – %	Proportion of employees receiving training in the last 13 weeks – %	Mean proportion of staff receiving off-the-job training – %	% of establishments employing 1 to 10	% of establishments employing 11 to 49	USA productivity lead over UK – %	SECTOR SKILLS COUNCILS whose footprint may include parts of this sector
Agriculture, hunting, forestry and fishing	1.3	28	13	16	90	9	89	Lantra
Mining and quarrying	*	*	31	*	74	18	-22	Proskills, Cogent Plus
Manufacturing	3.8	33	20	12	75	18	55	e-skills UK, SEMTA, Proskills, Cogent Plus, Food and Drink, Skillfast–UK
Electricity, gas and water supply	*	*	40	*	57	20	57	Energy and Utilities Skills
Construction	3.7	31	18	20	91	7	14	Construction Skills, SummitSkills
Wholesale and retail	2.5	30	21	15	85	12	55	Automotive Services, Skills for Logistics, Skillsmart, Lantra
Hotels and restaurants	33	29	24	15	77	20	31	Hospitality, SkillsactiveUK
Transport, storage and communication	4	27	22	14	82	12	14	Skills for Logistics, Go Skills, e-skills UK
Banking and insurance	3.8	48	37	28	71	22	59	Financial services
Real estate, renting and business activities	5.3	41	28	28	92	6	28	e-skills UK, Housing and Justice, Property, Construction Skills
Public administration, defence, compulsory social security	4.1	78	42	55	47	32	-16	Justice
Education	4.6	81	44	53	38	44	-16	Lifelong Learning
Health and social work	4.5	69	45	42	58	34	-16	Skills for Health, Social Care
Other services	3	35	25	21	90	8	-3	Skillset, SkillsactiveUK
Whole Economy	**3.7**	**37**	**29**	**22**	**83**	**13**	**31**	

Summary of Key Issues

BROAD SECTOR	Summary of Key Issues	SECTOR SKILLS COUNCILS whose footprint may include parts of this sector
Agriculture, hunting, forestry and fishing	• Low productivity compared to the USA • Ageing workforce and predominantly male • Dominance of small enterprises • Low levels of training • Workforce poorly qualified at levels 2/3+	Lantra
Mining and quarrying	• Ageing workforce and predominantly male • Skill shortages in some sub sectors	Proskills, Cogent Plus
Manufacturing	• Low productivity compared to international competitors especially in: petrochemicals; metals; electrical/electronic equipment; vehicles; textiles; wood products • Ageing workforce and predominantly male in some sub sectors • Significant skills shortages in skilled manual trades • Significant skill gaps especially in skilled manual trades and amongst operatives • Low levels of training	e-skills UK, SEMTA, Proskills, Cogent Plus, Food and Drink, Skillfast–UK
Electricity, gas and water supply	• Low productivity compared to international competition • Ageing workforce and predominantly male	Energy and Utilites Skills
Construction	• Ageing workforce and predominantly male • Dominance of small enterprises • Significant skill shortages especially in skilled manual trades • Low levels of training	Construction Skills, SummitSkills
Wholesale and retail	• Low productivity compared to international competition • Dominance of small enterprises • Significant skill gaps especially in sales/customer service staff • Low levels of training • Workforce poorly qualified at levels 2/3+	Automotive Services, Skills for Logistics, Skillsmart, Lantra
Hotels and restaurants	• Low productivity compared to international competition • Dominance of small enterprises • Significant skill gaps especially in sales/customer services • Low levels of training • Workforce poorly qualified at levels 2/3+	Hospitality, SkillsactiveUK
Transport, storage and communication	• Low productivity compared to international competitors in communications • Ageing workforce and predominantly male • Low levels of training • Workforce poorly qualified at levels 2/3+	Skills for Logistics, GoSkills, e-skills UK
Banking and insurance	• Low productivity compared to international competitors • Significant skill shortages especially in professional occupations; managers; administrative staff • Significant skill gaps especially in professional; administrative/secretarial; and sales and customer service staff	Financial Services

Sector			
Real estate, renting and business activities	• Low productivity compared to international competition • Dominance of small enterprises	• Significant skill shortages in professional and administrative/clerical occupations • Significant skill gaps in professional and administrative/clerical occupations	e-skills UK, Housing and Justice, Property, Construction Skills
Public administration, defence, compulsory social security	• Significant skill gaps especially in administrative/clerical occupations		Justice
Education	• Significant skill shortages especially in professional occupations		Lifelong Learning
Health and social work	• Significant skill shortages especially in associate professional/technical occupations and personal service occupations	• Significant skill gaps in professional; associate professional/technical; administrative; and personal service occupations	Skills for Health, Social Care
Other services	• Dominance of small enterprises		Skillset, SkillsactiveUK

Notes:

- For ease of presentation the economy is divided here into 14 sectors (NACE 1 Digit Sectors Classification) which is widely used internationally. Comparable regional level data is also available at this level of disaggregation. Further details can be found at www.ssdamatrix.org.uk
- NA – denotes where no such data is collected
- * – denotes where data is not available because of sample size and/or confidentiality
1 The columns do not add to 100 because the data is aggregated from the Sector Skills Matrix which presents data for 'no qualifications'; 'L1'; 'L2'; 'L3'; 'L4' and 'L5' separately. Data was not available in several of these categories for these sectors because of sample size and/or confidentiality.

Annex 4 Good Practice in Skills Development in Government and the Public Sector

Modern Apprenticeships	By the end of September 2004, the number of civil servants undertaking Modern Apprenticeships will be 28 per cent of all staff aged under 25 not qualified to level 2
Adult Basic Skills	Within the *Skills for Life* programme for improving adult literacy, language and numeracy skills, public sector staff were identified as a priority. 10,000 public sector workers will be helped by 2004
Leadership and Management	The Civil Service Management Board has asked a group of Permanent Secretaries and others from inside and outside the Civil Service to develop an action plan for developing successful leadership. Existing work to improve leadership and management skills across Government includes coaching and mentoring programmes and formal training courses
Union Learning Representatives	The Public and Commercial Services Union is introducing a project with the Department for Work and Pensions to develop a network of 1,000 Union Learning Representatives to help give its 85,000 members better access to learning opportunities
Foundation Degrees	The Home Office, in partnership with Portsmouth University, is offering a Foundation Degree in Policing Studies for Police Officers in Constabularies across England. The Department for Education and Skills is supporting work to develop a Foundation Degree for the Civil Service

Skills for Business Network	Proposals to establish Sector Skills Councils are well advanced in major areas of the public service, including health, justice, lifelong learning, and social care
Project Management	Recognising the growing importance of effective project and programme management for public sector staff, the DfES is working with the Association of Project Management to develop a nationally recognised project management qualification
Skills for the Health Service	The NHSU aims to offer NHS staff, who do not possess a higher education qualification, the opportunity to study through the NHSU towards a Foundation Degree. Working with Workforce Development Confederations and the LSC, it is also providing literacy, numeracy and English language support for increasing numbers of staff
Skills for the Police Service	There is a national strategy to promote learning in the Police Service. This sets priorities for training in the light of the National Skills Foresight Training Programme, and responds to the skills gaps and shortages identified by the Police Skills and Standards Organisation
Skills for the Armed Forces	The Ministry of Defence (MOD) sponsors armed forces personnel for Modern Apprenticeships and qualifications including National Vocational Qualifications and Foundation, Honours and Post-Graduate Degrees. The MOD has introduced mandatory basic skills screening for all new entrants. They will also be introducing an Enhanced Learning Credit scheme, enabling service personnel to get funding for further or higher education

Printed in the UK by The Stationery Office Limited
on behalf of the Controller of Her Majesty's Stationery Office
Id 147531   07/03

Annex 5 Response Form

We welcome your comments on the Skills Strategy. You may also wish to comment on the Regulatory Impact Assessment for the Skills Strategy. This is available on the Department for Education and Skills website at **www.dfes.gov.uk/ria**

The information you send to the Department for Education and Skills may be shared with colleagues within the Department. It may be published as part of a summary of comments made on the White Paper. We will assume that you are content for us to do this. If you are replying by e-mail, your consent overrides any confidentiality disclaimer that is generated by your organisation's information technology system. If you do not wish your comments to be published as part of a summary, then please request this in the main text of your response.

The Department may, in accordance with the Code of Practice on Access to Government Information, make available on public request, individual responses. This does include your comments unless you tell us that you wish them to remain confidential.

Please insert 'X' if you want to keep your response confidential ☐

Name

Organisation (if applicable)

Address

If you have any enquiries about this form or the Skills Strategy, please contact the Public Enquiry Unit:

Telephone: **0870 000 2288** Email: **info@dfes.gsi.gov.uk**

Please insert 'X' in **one** of the following boxes that best describes you as a respondent.

☐	National Organisation	☐	Employer
☐	Work Based Learning Provider	☐	College or Training Provider
☐	Trade Union	☐	Learning and Skills Council
☐	Individual	☐	Voluntary Organisation
☐	Local Education Authority	☐	Regional Body
☐	Representative body	☐	School
☐	Sectoral Body	☐	Higher Education Institution
☐	Other (please specify)		

We welcome your comments on the Skills Strategy. You may also wish to comment on the Regulatory Impact Assessment for the Skills Strategy. This is available on the Department for Education and Skills website at **www.dfes.gov.uk/ria**

Comments:

Thank you for taking the time to let us have your views. We do not normally acknowledge receipt of individual responses unless you tick the box below.

Please acknowledge this reply

At the Department for Education and Skills we carry out research and consult on a range of education and skills topics. Your views are valuable to us. Please indicate using the boxes below if you would be happy for us to contact you again, from time to time, either for research purposes or to send you consultation documents.

Yes   No

Please send completed responses to the address shown below by **31 October 2003**.

Send by post to: **Consultation Unit, Department for Education and Skills, Level 1b, Castle View House, East Lane, Runcorn, WA7 2GJ.**

Or by e-mail to: **SkillsStrategy.comments@dfes.gsi.gov.uk**